HOPE

CONQUERS ALL

HOPE
CONQUERS ALL

Inspiring Stories of Love and
Healing from CaringBridge

SONA MEHRING

**CENTER
STREET**

New York Boston Nashville

Center Street
Hachette Book Group
237 Park Avenue
New York, NY 10017

www.CenterStreet.com

Printed in the United States of America

RRD-C

First edition: August 2013
10 9 8 7 6 5 4 3 2 1

Center Street is a division of Hachette Book Group, Inc.
The Center Street name and logo are trademarks of Hachette Book Group, Inc.

The Hachette Speakers Bureau provides a wide range of authors for speaking events. To find out more, go to www.HachetteSpeakersBureau.com or call (866) 376-6591.

The publisher is not responsible for websites (or their content) that are not owned by the publisher.

Library of Congress Control Number: 2013939376

To my mother, Bonnie, who lived a life of care-giving

To Brighid and her parents, JoAnn and Darrin,
and her siblings Sepp, Anya, and Gabriel

Contents

CONTENTS

Foreword

I remember the moment well. It was a few weeks after I was diagnosed in 2004 with mantle cell lymphoma, a deadly form of non-Hodgkin's lymphoma. I was in a bad way, less physically than emotionally. I couldn't rouse myself out of the fog of my own condition. I thought I might die, or at least suffer horribly during treatment, and I couldn't bear to talk about it on the phone to family, friends, and especially that group of people somewhere between friends and acquaintances, whom I liked well enough but with whom I simply didn't have the physical or emotional energy to chat. Being cheerful on the phone or with visitors was one more burden than I could bear. I'm a gregarious person by nature, but I began not answering the phone. Even e-mail was a problem. I couldn't possibly answer all of it, but felt terrible that I wasn't thanking people individually and that their greetings went unacknowledged. Then I felt terrible for feeling terrible about it, which was a problem because I wasn't feeling so hot in the first place.

Just as my annoyance and guilty feeling about not being in touch began to weigh on me, my sister Jennifer told me about

CaringBridge.org. At first I didn't quite understand the idea. It was social networking before anyone called it that. Once she set up the account for me, I found it to be one of the best developments of an otherwise terrible time. The website was often the vehicle for the emotional sustenance I so desperately needed.

Some of the posted messages were straightforward words of sympathy and encouragement; others made me laugh out loud. My friend Gregg wrote hilarious riffs about politics that had nothing to do with my illness. Another guy named Steve was someone I hadn't seen since freshman year in high school more than thirty years earlier. We weren't really friends then, but through CaringBridge and his insightful posts, we became friends. Colleagues from work had a way to stay in touch during my several months at home. My children and even my mother-in-law wrote amusing things that consistently cheered me up. I saw hidden talents for writing and sides of various people in my life that I hadn't known before. Through the course of my illness, hundreds of people were in touch, and I appreciated every one of them. Occasionally I would write a long reply, often singling people out by name. But I was able to do this when I wanted to, not when the phone happened to ring.

My sister and my wife and others in my family posted updates on my medical condition as I underwent a successful bone marrow transplant. But I could also do some of that myself—at my leisure, on my own terms, wrapped in a cocoon of love.

My friend, Garry Trudeau, went on the site and soon his *Doonesbury* comic strip incorporated CaringBridge. B.D., the football-helmeted character who was one of the original characters in the strip, goes to fight in Iraq, where he loses the helmet and a limb. He returns for a long convalescence, during which he stays in touch with friends through CaringBridge.org. My colleagues at NBC News ran a story on *NBC Nightly News* about the site, and I have become almost evangelical about spreading word of CaringBridge to anyone I know who is ailing or might have someone in the family who needs this lifeline. In the years since I was sick, I've posted messages for scores of friends and acquaintances who have set up accounts. Facebook, by the way, cannot perform the same function. The communities created there are not as focused on the patient. CaringBridge isn't just about staying in touch; it's about staying in touch for a specific humane purpose.

I hope anyone reading this will help spread the word to patients, medical professionals (who should tell all patients about the site), and anyone else who might benefit from this wonderful new institution in our lives.

—Jonathan Alter

Introduction

How the Legacy of One Baby
Inspired Hope for Millions

In May 1997, when my close friend, JoAnn, was hospitalized with a life-threatening pregnancy, I asked her husband, Darrin, what I could do to help. Overwhelmed and exhausted, he said, "Just let everyone know what's going on." As soon as I hung up, I started dialing, but after just a handful of emotionally charged calls, I felt drained and exhausted myself. Scanning the long list of people who needed to be contacted, I thought, *There's got to be a better way to keep people informed.*

Given my background as a web design and technology consultant, I naturally turned to the Internet. In a matter of hours, I had created a website where I could post regular updates, and where family and friends could leave messages in a guest book. On June 7, the day that Brighid was born three months prematurely, the first CaringBridge site was born as well. Sadly, after a nine-day struggle against tremendous odds, Brighid died in surgery. I posted the heart-wrenching news on Brighid's site along with a final message from JoAnn and Darrin thanking family and friends for their love and support.

That first CaringBridge site was a blessing to everyone involved. JoAnn and Darrin were relieved of the crushing burden of regularly updating dozens of friends and loved ones who desperately wanted to know what was going on but didn't want to intrude during a family health crisis. With their communication needs taken care of, JoAnn and Darrin could focus their time and emotional energy on what mattered most.

As Brighid's site took on a life of its own, I felt a lightning bolt of inspiration pierce my heart and soul. When that precious little girl lost her battle for life, I knew I couldn't let the concept die along with Brighid. Attending her memorial service only added to the urgency of my newfound mission. The waves of love and support that had surged through the Internet to comfort Brighid's parents were vividly embodied by the sea of caring people who came together to mourn and pay their respects. To my surprise, dozens of people approached me to express their gratitude for keeping them informed and giving them the ability to directly support JoAnn and Darrin. I left feeling even more inspired, knowing that rolling out CaringBridge was no longer a choice but a calling.

The name CaringBridge rose organically out of "caring for Brighid." It also struck me as ideal because it served as a bridge of caring between Brighid's parents and their concerned friends and loved ones. Indeed, it was not only a bridge but a lifeline.

Since I had manually programmed Brighid's site in HTML, my first priority was making the interface user-friendly and accessible to everyone. It took me eight weeks to create a standalone service that enabled people to easily create a private, personal site and fill in the content themselves. Without realizing it at the time, I had pioneered the concept of personal-health social networking. As word of this new resource began spreading, other families immersed in difficult medical journeys found their way to CaringBridge.

At the time, I looked at CaringBridge as a pro bono community service provided by Beacon Point Technologies, the consulting company I had founded in 1995. Over the next two years, however, as CaringBridge steadily grew, it consumed more and more of my time, focus, and resources. My appreciation for the power of CaringBridge to facilitate the exchange of information, love, and support during serious health challenges grew exponentially when I created sites for my ninety-four-year-old grandma, Bessie, and for my mother, Bonnie, who was diagnosed with Stage IV breast cancer in 1998. In 2001, I reactivated my mother's site when she was stricken with liver cancer, which took her life that year. Those intensely emotional firsthand experiences spurred me on even more. I remember thinking, *This needs to be out there and I need to be the one doing it.*

My dedication to the care and growth of CaringBridge soon eclipsed my interest in the other Internet services my company offered. In 2002, still without a proven revenue model, I followed the advice of Frank Forsberg, a senior executive at United Way and a founding board member of CaringBridge, who told me, "Jump and the net will appear." I quickly wrapped up my Beacon Point projects, referred my clients elsewhere, and turned my attention full-time to CaringBridge. With the help of a growing number of dedicated volunteers, we began bringing in enough charitable donations to be self-sustaining by the end of 2003. Although I explored other potential revenue streams, it never felt right to rely solely on corporate funding. Today, 90 percent of donations come from individual charitable giving. That allows us to keep the families touched by CaringBridge at the center of what we do.

Since its inception, hundreds of thousands of CaringBridge sites have gone live, generating billions of site visits. Every day, CaringBridge brings together more than half a million people. Seven years before the arrival of Facebook, CaringBridge demonstrated that the Internet could be a potent tool for building online social communities that connect people in authentic and meaningful ways.

Both figuratively and literally, CaringBridge is a lifesaver. Turning to CaringBridge not only eases a family's communication burden, it also can have a profound effect on a patient's emotional and physical health and well-being. Whether a patient is coping with cancer, a stroke, heart disease, a difficult pregnancy, or a traumatic accident, sharing their journey—the highs and lows, the hopes and fears—with friends and loved ones is both calming and healing. As Tom Ferguson, MD, founder of e-patients.net, noted, "An individual's social network...has long been recognized as an important factor in maintaining health and managing disease more effectively."

Taking a leap of faith in CaringBridge has also deepened my spiritual path in ways both practical and profound. Not a day goes by that I don't feel blessed to know that the work I do brings comfort, love, and strength to others in their hour of need. I have always enjoyed working with people and technology, but the opportunity to work at something that so powerfully and positively impacts people's lives takes me from "enjoyment" to "joyous."

CaringBridge as an organization has also been blessed, although I can't pretend to explain the force that seems to be guiding us with infinite patience and wisdom. Opportunities to advance the good we do in the world consistently and surprisingly present themselves. I have a big appetite for consuming information and following trends at the three-way intersection between health care, technology, and nonprofit, and am always looking for ways to reach more people and serve them better. We have stayed relevant by actively soliciting feedback from users and updating the site regularly. Ultimately, our Compassion Technology™ enables CaringBridge to fulfill its mission of amplifying the love, hope, and compassion in the world, making each health journey easier to bear.

In our office, there is a large CaringBridge History Map that begins with Brighid's birth. It reminds us every day why we do the work that we do. I am humbled and awed to know that, despite her short life, Brighid has made a difference in the lives of millions of people around the globe. I consider this book another chapter in her legacy of love. May these stories touch your heart as they touched mine.

—Sona Mehring

HOPE

CONQUERS ALL

CARRIE MURCHISON

You've Got to Know When You're "In It"

We were living our lives, working our big jobs in Washington, DC. We had a little dream house with an American flag outside, and a cute new baby. We'd just returned from having the baby baptized in Dallas, where my husband, Will, grew up, and where I'd lived before my family moved to Houston when I was small. I was looking at pictures of the baptism, and although I'm no fashion model, I kept thinking that I looked really ugly. I couldn't put my finger on it, but something about my appearance was strange.

I don't look in the mirror much. I've always had a "one chance" philosophy about makeup: you get one shot in the morning and that's it for the rest of the day. And at the time, I was still losing my baby weight, so why depress myself? But I found the closest mirror and couldn't believe what I saw: my nostrils were almost completely sideways. My *entire nose* had twisted. Somehow my nostrils ran parallel to one another instead of perpendicular. Something was pushing them seriously out of alignment. I rushed into the bedroom in a panic and confronted Will. "Have you noticed my nose, Will? Look at my nostrils. They're completely sideways!"

"Well, yeah," he said, confusion written all over his face. "Now that you mention it. That's really weird."

Will is one of those guys who doesn't notice, or at least doesn't comment, if you've gained fifteen pounds. Of course, it sucks if you've *lost* fifteen pounds and he doesn't notice, but it's always good on the way up.

We went to a plastic surgeon. He poked and prodded and diagnosed my problem as an "innocent" cyst. "I can drain this right here in the office if you want," he said, "but typically these things tend to fill themselves back up. I think everyone would be more comfortable if we scheduled you for outpatient surgery and took it out."

I thought nothing of it. While our son was in day care, Will took the day off from work and drove me to and from the procedure. I came home with a big bandage on my face.

Several days later, I went to the surgeon by myself to get the dressings removed. But the surgeon had me come into his office instead of the exam room. Suddenly I had the growing sense that my wonderful, kind doctor with the loving bedside manner was about to deliver bad news. He put his arm around me, smiled gently, and said, "I love you, kiddo."

"So…"

"You threw us for a real loop on this one," he said. "It wasn't what we thought it would be."

First thought: it's cancer.

"It's cancer," he said. "But the problem is that the pathologists who've looked at this can't agree on what kind of cancer."

"What does that mean?" I asked, sinking into a chair. I didn't know whether to cry or be sick. Or both.

"All we know is that it's some sort of malignant spindle cell neoplasm."

"A what?"

He explained that *spindle cell* typically refers to a "rapidly reproducing" cancer, which meant that the cancer wasn't a local phenomenon. Although they'd only done one small day surgery to remove a tumor, he and the pathologists assumed that the cancer had probably already spread.

It seems almost funny in hindsight, but at the time, my first thought was that the diagnosis was inconvenient. Bad timing. Not because it meant that I was very sick but because Will and I had just put our house on the market. After ten years in DC, we wanted to move back to Texas. I told the doctor and asked him what we should do. "Sweetie," he said, "you'll probably be spending the next year of your life in a medical center. If you, say, choose to go to Houston, you'll be in an apartment near MD Anderson Cancer Center." The way he said it felt like he meant the *final* year of my life.

And that was it, except for waiting to find out exactly what my cancer was. As the mystery tumor was flown around the world for inspection, I spent the next two weeks thinking, *Wow, I cannot believe my life is over.* My sister flew in from Houston. I began boxing my clothes to give away to Goodwill. I figured if I was going to die, I didn't want to leave a heavy load to deal with if I didn't come back. I didn't want my skinny husband to see the size of my fat jeans after I was gone.

I was no stranger to cancer. My Grandmother Tierney, an amazing angel still alive at ninety-five, was a breast cancer survivor in her sixties, a premature widow, and an adoring mother who raised a handicapped son into his sixties and then buried not one but two adult children. One of them was my mother, Margo, who was diagnosed with brain cancer when she was only thirty-six years old. The doctors gave her eight months to live. Somehow, she survived for seventeen more years, but for most intents and purposes her life was over at thirty-six. She entered a nursing home at forty-six, and died when she was fifty-four, shortly before my wedding. Her hair never grew back. She gained a hundred pounds. She had no energy. Long gone was the vibrant woman we'd all known. Her loss was profound.

And then, just when I was convinced that I'd finally gotten to lead the perfect life I'd always dreamed of, I get cancer when I'm thirty-two?! Are you kidding me? The whole family just went, "Here we go again."

I worked on getting fast-tracked into MD Anderson, a widely respected treatment center and one of three places in the world that had a specialized radiation therapy for my type of cancer. They told me I had to be there within two weeks; it was that critical. I didn't have time to do an Internet search for places to stay, so thank goodness my older sister, Jennifer, still lived in Houston and offered Will and me and our son free lodging. Most of my cancer-fighting comrades don't get that lucky. I had a family support network and I wasn't reluctant to use it. Will arranged to do his job remotely.

Just before the family left for Houston, I got a bit of good news. The Mayo Clinic had examined my biopsy and determined that it was not spindle cell. Instead, I had a fibrosarcoma, a cousin of spindle cell cancer. It was cancer, and it was still serious, but my tumor was much less likely to violently spread.

My fibrosarcoma was rare—less than one percent of all

cancers—and is typically found in the fatty part of one's thigh or biceps. Had the fibrosarcoma actually been in my thigh, I might never have noticed it. The blessing and the curse of having the tumor in my skull is that it was like sticking a lima bean in my nose. I noticed it instead of just dropping dead one day.

In Houston, I got less good news: prepare for a series of "disfiguring surgeries" that would occur over the next year. Usually the doctors remove a roughly two-inch-diameter piece around the tumor. However, a two-inch-diameter excision meant I'd lose my nose, and they'd have to rebuild it. I'd always cared a lot about my appearance, but I remember lying in bed one night, praying to God, "Please, please, please make me a disfigured woman."

I guess that's what having a dream husband and child will do. I wanted to survive at any cost.

———

My first night at MD Anderson was one of the worst. I was scheduled for a series of scans, but I had no idea that an MRI was equivalent to being buried alive. Being ignorant, I didn't request the Ativan to help me get through the claustrophobia. The technicians just put a weight on my chest and packed me up like a mummy. I couldn't move my arms. My head was in a face cage. I had something on my nose. They put a little balloon in my hand and, as I slid into the tunnel, someone said, "If you have an emergency, press this balloon." I pressed it the moment I got in there. "I can't do it! I can't do it!" They pulled me out. I got the Ativan, and tried again—this time successfully.

Will and my sister were in the room to witness everything. It's unusual, but Will got to stay because he's my husband, and although Jennifer didn't have to be there, in a testament to how much she loves me, she stayed by my side despite being warned that her intrauterine contraceptive device would be rendered ineffective or possibly dislodged by magnetic force if exposed to the MRI machine. She said, "I don't care if it flies out of my wazoo! I want to be in here with my sister!"

To my surprise that turned out to be the great turning point in the relationship between my sister and my husband—the two most important people in my life. They had always had mutual respect, but they're very different personality types and hadn't had a full appreciation for each other before. Having this shared fear and love brought them together. Good thing, because we were all roommates for three months.

My father, who also lives in Houston, was there that night, too, though not at the MRI. He's six foot seven and three hundred and something pounds. While waiting for the technicians to whisk me off to the scans, he excused himself to go to the bathroom. He came back moments later in tears. "Ugh. The smell of that bathroom brings back so many memories," he said. He meant memories of my mother's cancer. I guess the pain never goes away.

Will somehow remained calm, to a fault. In fact, for some reason, during the two weeks between getting diagnosed and leaving for Houston, his parents never "got the memo" that I had cancer. I still give him a hard time about it. "Remember that time you *forgot* to tell your parents I had cancer?" I still don't know whether it was denial or oblivion or a coping mechanism, or a swirl of all three. I can't help but wear my heart and emotions on my sleeve. Will is the strong, silent type. At times I needed what I'd expect from a girlfriend, who validates your feelings instead of trying to find solutions. But I suppose if Will and I had both acted out the panic that I was in, all hell would have broken loose. Instead, Will remained optimistic and reassuring while I'd tremble in my bed at night. I remember looking down and seeing my toes literally shaking at the thought of *I cannot believe I am going to leave this precious husband and child.* He'd just hold me and say, "Everything's going to be fine."

Some days that attitude was useful. Other days I wanted to punch him.

After the scans, Will and I met with Dr. Hannah, our amazing oncologist, to get the results. It's no understatement to say that we expected the worst news of our lives. Instead, we got great news. "We couldn't find any cancer. Not anywhere in your body. Apparently your plastic surgeon did a really good job." We were bowled over. I may have asked Dr. Hannah to repeat that once or ten times.

"Even so," he continued, "the tumor site doesn't have clear margins. But whatever remains is so microscopic that it's not being picked up by the scans."

"What does that mean?" I asked. "Do I still have cancer?"

"It means you could walk away and have about a fifty-fifty shot of not dying from this," he explained. "Or you could do thirty-two rounds of radiation and increase your chances to more like seventy-five to ninety percent."

That was a no-brainer.

Good news, bad news, a cautiously optimistic prognosis, an uncertain future. It's tough for anyone, but honestly for me it wasn't the toughest time of my life. And the strength I drew from the past helped confront the present.

For a couple of years when I was in high school, my mom was really sick. A large branch of our family was quite wealthy, but my dad was the branch of the family that never became wealthy. We had lived in a nice enough neighborhood, but then our house was foreclosed on before *foreclosure* was a word everyone knew. With my sister in college, my mom and I moved into a little apartment, when, in pure peer-pressure terms, the people in my crowd didn't live in apartments. I was seventeen. To pay the bills, I worked two jobs. I interned at a state senator's radio talk show during the day and managed a restaurant at night. I didn't go to prom because I had to work that evening. I'd come home at eleven o'clock at night and find my mom asleep on the living room couch with a bowl of cold cereal and newspapers scattered around her. She had just started to become incontinent, but no one recognized that she was sick again. It was awful. Those were truly my darkest, darkest days, so dark that, to be perfectly honest, I truly understand what it's like to be suicidal.

The only reason I didn't kill myself is that my precious grandmother Tierney was alive. With all she'd been through—and would go through in the future—she has a fantastic, glass-half-full attitude toward life. I didn't hold out much hope for myself, but I couldn't bear for her to suffer another heartbreak.

Fortunately, she wasn't the only one in my corner. I remember complaining to my mom's best friend, Bonnie. "I can't ever go to college," I moaned. "I'm trying to help my mom pay for her apartment. There's no way."

"You are Carrie Langdon," she said. "Of course you're going to college."

I guess she saw something I couldn't, and it inspired me. I'd never given myself much credit. I'd grown up around these gorgeous, perfect, beautiful friends and always felt like the ugly duckling. I couldn't picture myself getting married, and if I did, not to a cute guy. I couldn't picture owning a half-million-dollar home. I couldn't picture having a wonderful baby—even though all I ever wanted was to be a mother.

Bonnie's certainty was a seed of hope and I let it grow. I worked my ass off, got scholarships, and paid my way through college at the University of Texas. Near the end of senior year, when I told my sister that I wanted to seek my fortune in Washington, DC, but had no money, she bought me a plane ticket.

"Go up at spring break and come home with a job," she said. "This is your one shot." Jennifer was only three and a half years older, but she'd become like my mother. I did what I had to do. Karl Rove was one of my teachers for a seminar, and he wrote me a recommendation for a job on Capitol Hill. I flew to DC and did everything short of taping my résumé on the wall. I got a job. Rove's recommendation is probably why I ended up in the office of Congress's most conservative member.

A job was great, but I hadn't graduated yet, so I went back to the University of Texas and met individually with each of my professors to convince them that they should calculate my grade to allow me to graduate without taking a final. I explained that I had a very important job in the US House of Representatives. That was my first real act of lobbying, and they let me out of the finals. I went back to DC and worked six weeks for the congressman—which turned out to be answering the phone and taking sweaty constituents on tours of the Capitol—before the congressman flew me home for the weekend to graduate, and then back to continue the job.

That's the kind of determination that my sister and I have always had, and it helped me deal with my cancer. Sometimes I think the most perfect way to grow up is surrounded by wealth, privilege, and opportunity—and have none of it yourself. My sister and I are who we are because we had no safety net. All we saw were people around us who lived the lives we wanted to have for ourselves.

I managed to make it happen. I worked on Capitol Hill for a few years, for $20,000 a year. Once I had all the contacts and had learned the legislative process, I got to graduate to lobbying. For a year after I left the Hill I wrote an advice column for Hill staffers called "Dear Carrie." That was my first entrepreneurial gig, a cross between "Roll Call" and "Ann Landers." I enjoyed being a little local celebrity. I'd get to answer questions like: "I've been on a few dates with a lobbyist who gave me a Christmas gift that exceeds the gift limit. How should I tactfully return it?"

Afterward I went to work in the government relations office for International Paper for about four years. Then I went to work for eBay. I tracked federal, state, and international legislation and ran a network of about a quarter million people who are eBay buyers and sellers. When various legislation got to the point where we needed to weigh in, I'd write letters, send them out to my network, and launch a giant grassroots campaign on issues like Internet neutrality and Internet sales tax legislation.

Along the way I met and fell in love with Will. When we were babies, we lived next door to each other in Dallas, before my family moved away. My father said that if we'd both had remote-controlled televisions, we could have changed one another's channels. Twenty years later, after I'd left, I got an e-mail from a friend in the congressman's office saying, "Hey, guess what? There's a new guy in the office."

"Is he cute?????" I wrote back.

"Yeah, but he's not your type. He's skinny and quiet."

It turned out that he was my type. For our fifth wedding anniversary I made a video retracing our paths to each other. In the video I said, "The congressman thought we were a good match. I wasn't so sure. Then came a party, and a kiss...that went unacknowledged for six months. And so began our 'courtship'...."

I was on the verge of getting everything I'd dreamed of when I was seventeen, and thanks to Grandma Tierney, I knew it when it happened. She gave me a gift that still keeps on giving: the ability to recognize when you're "in it."

Now, there was no way I'd let all of this end from cancer.

I'd come so far from 1994.

I've always been a real open book. Will and I had to get out of DC so quickly and were in such turmoil that we hardly had time to tell people what was going on. I was horrified to think that somebody important to us might not hear the story for a long time. CaringBridge was a way to get the word out in a capacity I could handle, since at the time my capacity was basically zero.

My sister wrote most of the early posts, and I knew that the information would go quasi-viral through our personal network. In fact, I didn't write in my CaringBridge journal until near the end because I was busy going to cancer treatments every day. The radiation makes you tired. I was on lots of drugs. I had to take care of a baby I'd just weaned. And I'm a complete masochist. I was determined to maintain my full-time eBay job, from a satellite office in Houston. No wonder I was physically and emo-tionally exhausted.

CaringBridge helped there, too. Every time I got a warm, compassionate e-mail from someone during my treatment, I felt like it was warm and compassionate and thoughtful for about five minutes—and then I was super stressed out about when I'd have the time to respond to all the e-mails pouring in. I chalked it up to my mother being a real stickler for all correspondence, specifically thank-you notes. But when anyone wrote a similarly beautiful message on my CaringBridge guest book—"Whatever you need, whenever you need it," "You are an amazing woman and this frightening chapter of your life will soon be just another story from your past that speaks of your grace and strength of character," "Your endurance and attitude have been an inspira-tion to us all"—I felt *only* the loving part and not the stress part. It sounds selfish, but CaringBridge made it possible for me to take a pass and let people communicate with me in a one-way fashion. And often, on my darkest days, I would just refresh and refresh the guest book and hope that somebody else had written.

I feel I should credit my religious faith for the inspiration and strength that got me through the crisis, but that's not what authentically comes to mind. It's more my tribe. My family. Cancer's gift was that it threw me back into the community that had raised me. Even though I'd had a dysfunctional childhood, I was at the same time surrounded by amazing women, who were my mom's best friends, most of them the mothers of my girl-friends. They were my angels.

My mother's best friend Bonnie, to whom I'd complained

about not being able to go to college, took me for my treatments when I came back to Houston. One day we were on our way home from the hospital and we went to the drive-through for a milk shake. Suddenly, Bonnie started crying. I asked her why. "Oh my gosh," she said, wiping at the tears. "I used to take your mom here for a milk shake after her treatments."

I had a checkup two weeks ago that marked four years since discovering the cancer. Next year will be the big anniversary, the five-year mark when your chances of a reoccurrence drop, and long-term chances of survival go up. Initially, I got checkups every three months, which is why we moved permanently back to Texas, to be close to my doctors. I also still wanted to work, and since there was an eBay office in Austin, my boss was happy to let me work remotely.

Eventually, I left my eBay job and came out of the closet as a graphic designer, which has long been my true passion. I wanted to do professionally what I had been doing for friends—and myself on the side—for years: invitations and stationery.

I also decided to use my business to help CaringBridge by donating a percentage of my profits. My tagline is "Celebrating Life," and it fits, because most of what I'm doing is celebration stuff—people's birthdays, baby showers, weddings, anniversaries. It also has a deeper meaning. Thanks to Grandma Tierney, *I know I'm in it*. It's so amazing that I have my life and I'm able to do what I love every day.

It feels egotistical to say, "I want to be an inspiration," but I do. When I was in treatment, and still to this day, I only want to hear success stories. I don't care if you call that naive. If I can be a success story and help anybody going through what I went through, I want them to know that it's possible to make it to the other side.

A Proven Way to Get Help

When you're at the height of receiving medical care, or feeling run-down or exhausted from everything life throws at you, it's not unusual to find yourself going it alone.

It can happen during a health journey or at some other critical moment in your life, and most often, the reason is simple: when you need help, you have to ask.

There are always people who care and want to be there to support you, but they either don't know that you need help, don't know what they can do, or aren't sure how to help.

Don't be afraid to ask for help, and be specific. In the same way that any organization—a school, church, or nonprofit—offers a variety of ways volunteers can pitch in, share a list of ways your family and friends can help. Use an online planner or service to coordinate sign-ups.

The people around you will be more likely to lend a hand if they know exactly what you need.

LISA FOTO

It's Me...

I opened my eyes to find myself in a bed. A woman—a stranger—stood over me, her young face close to mine, and asked me softly if I knew what year it was. I stared at her, but said nothing. I needed to clear my head. The last thing I remembered was exercising at the gym, wearing blue booties over my tennis shoes, my hands on the ground like in a racer's starting stance, running in place on a slippery whiteboard. I didn't like that exercise, but I was trying to increase my endurance, and my trainer was pushing me hard. Suddenly, I felt a sharp pain near my right ear and the world went blank.

Now I was terrified. I wondered, *Why is she asking me that? What if I don't know the year?* "I don't like your question," I finally said.

"Why not?" she asked, and stood straight up. I could see from her uniform that she was a nurse. I quickly looked down at myself. I was in a hospital bed. Tubes ran across and under the covers, and some ended in my arms.

"What if my answer is wrong?"

"Let's find out before you get upset." She smiled to encourage me, but her eyes remained intent, searching.

I pressed my lips together, stalling for time, while my chest pounded. "I think it's...2007."

"That's right!" she said.

"Then why did you ask me that?"

Her answer was another question: "Who's the president of the United States?"

"Look. Am I dying?" I asked.

"You're not dying."

"Well, these are the questions they ask you in the movies when you're dying."

"We just want to know if you're in there," she replied.

"Of course I'm in here!" I snapped. "Isn't there a better question, like, 'What day is today?'"

"Do you know?"

"Obviously not. But I'd like to."

"It's April eighteenth."

April 18th? I'd gone to the gym on March 20th. I'd been in the middle of planning my second daughter's wedding. "April? You mean I've missed Easter? I...I've missed my...wedding anniversary."

"Yes," the nurse said kindly. "But think about how happy your husband is going to be because you remembered."

She was right. "But I still didn't like your questions," I said, closing my eyes again.

Soon my family flooded into the room, overjoyed: my husband, John; my children Amanda, Jessica, and Kyle. Together they praised God, welcomed me back, and told me what had happened while I was away.

I'd been working with my trainer, Terry, when I had what he thought was a seizure, and lost consciousness. He called 911. An ambulance rushed me to Saddleback Hospital. Later, the EMT told me that I came to briefly on the way, and kept trying to sit up while grabbing my head and saying how much it hurt. I didn't know it then, but I knew the EMT. Her father was our TV repairman and she'd recognized my name on the gym chart. By the grace of God, she also paid attention to my complaint of head pain and called in for an immediate CAT scan at Saddleback. They discovered that I'd had a massive brain hemorrhage. An aneurysm—which is a weakened artery—had ruptured, causing a bleed deep in my brain. A Level 5, the most serious.

But why me? I was forty-seven and had no history of health problems. I'd never even had a headache. Apparently that meant nothing. All along I'd had the aneurysm lurking, waiting. When I overexerted myself on the whiteboard, my blood pressure went too high, and like a balloon with too much air in it, the artery popped.

Saddleback didn't even check me in, preferring instead to transfer me to Mission Hospital, because they could better handle my critical condition with a new procedure called an endovascular coil. The EMT called Mission's trauma line, and the nurse there *also* knew me. She orchestrated the whole surgical team to wait for my arrival, and they rushed me into surgery. The vascular-intervention radiologist there saved my life.

At the time, the coil was a very aggressive, cutting-edge treatment. You have to be on the operating table within an hour of your collapse. The traditional practice was to open the skull, pull the brain apart, find the bleed, clean out the blood, and clip it off. The coiling procedure doesn't use clips. They don't even cut into your head. The coils are actually small platinum threads shot through the femoral artery to the bleed, where they form a ball of "yarn" that gets big enough to plug the hole.

Some people would say I had incredible luck. I think God

determined everything, all the "coincidences," because He cared about me and wanted me taken to a safe place. It's hard for me to understand how it could have been otherwise.

―――――――

I didn't wake up in recovery. The doctor used pentobarbital to induce a coma so my brain and body had the maximum opportunity to heal. He wanted no stimulation. No bright lights. No loud talking, noises, or music. To help me breathe, I was hooked up to a ventilator. The ICU monitored me for possible brain swelling. For the first few days I was stable, but then my brain began to expand beyond an ability to control it with medication. I had an emergency craniotomy to remove a horseshoe-shaped piece of my skull, which allowed my brain tissue to swell unimpeded without increasing the pressure.

The most critical phase of postrupture recovery is days four through fourteen. In response to the bleed, blood vessels can contract and cut off crucial oxygen. These contractions are called vasospasms and, if uncontrolled, can result in an ischemic stroke. To prevent this I had surgery again to drill a hole in the top of my head into which a monitor was inserted and pushed into my brain to measure the oxygen level. A dip in the level was an early warning of a vasospasm, and the ICU team would rush me to have an angiogram to determine the location. Using the femoral artery again, medication was sent to the specific area to get the blood vessels to relax. I had nineteen angiograms. Usually twice a day.

After a week in the ICU, the coma-inducing pentobarbital was withdrawn. I wouldn't wake up immediately, the doctor cautioned. It could still take weeks. In fact, as my vasospasms

continued, I had to be sedated for the angiograms, which inter-
fered with my breathing. I had begun to breathe on my own,
but now I needed a tracheostomy and the ventilation hookup inserted through a hole in my throat. I also got a feeding tube put
directly into my stomach, with a second tube to drain stomach
acid.

When the vasospasms stopped and my blood vessels were
clear, the doctor wanted to wake me. He ordered all invasive
monitoring tubes removed. My lungs were scoped for infection
and came back clean. I went on a methadone protocol to wean
me from the morphine and Ativan I'd also gotten for twenty-
three days. I still needed to conserve all my strength to work
through my therapies and to breathe on my own again, but a
nurse or doctor would shake me and although I'd open my eyes,
I was still nonresponsive. Or I just didn't remember. One day
my son, Kyle, said, "Hey Mom, can you open your eyes?" and
to everyone's surprise I nodded my head. Kyle asked again, "You
can?!?" Again, a slight nod. My daughter Amanda said, "Then do
it!!" And I did! But when my husband, John, asked me to pucker
up for a kiss, I didn't. I'm told he kissed me anyway and that the
edges of my mouth turned up in a smile.

My return to full awareness was agonizingly slow for my
family. Yet, as I would soon discover, every day they filled my
CaringBridge journal with reports, praised God, and made specific prayer requests to help me surmount every obstacle and best
every challenge. Trying to communicate with me must have been
difficult and confusing, but they never gave up. And slowly but
surely I came back to life.

While I couldn't remember anything since my hemorrhage,
my coma was not a blank and empty experience. I didn't see
any white light, but I had what later seemed to me to be vivid

dreams. When my brain heard doctors being paged, I had imagined the voices were the PA system at an airport where I was trying to catch a flight to a horse show. I also heard a Bee Gees song, but in my dream I was on the phone, on hold. I recall being vaguely annoyed because the song was a little too upbeat. I also imagined that I was pregnant; that must have been when they did ultrasounds.

Doctors will tell you that in cases like mine, patients often wake up anxious, even angry, and want to pull all the lines out of their arms and elsewhere. Not me. I recall being upset only once, when I wanted to get out of bed to use the bathroom. I had grown very tired of the bedpan. My husband later told me that I'd asked him, "How much is this hotel anyway."

"Ten thousand a day," he said.

"Well, for ten thousand dollars a day," I said, "you'd think you could get a bathroom."

After I woke up, I immediately began acute rehab. My doctor wanted me to eat with others and not hide in my room, and he told the ICU staff to wheel me down to breakfast. I passed the open door of the computer room on the way, and I asked to be brought there after eating. My family had told me about the CaringBridge journal they'd established for me, and now I wanted to read it for myself.

The story of my illness and what my family had been through, posted by my daughter Amanda, my friend Jackie, and my husband, John, was almost too much to absorb. It was like a Mack truck had run over the family. John was thrust into making life-and-death decisions for me. My parents had come to support him, as had my brother and sister and their families. Even my ex-husband (and father of my three children) was there. When he was six, his father had died from a brain aneurysm at the age of thirty-two. At the outset no one thought I would make it, but they filled the journal with prayers—and those prayers had worked.

I read all the guest-book messages and discovered one that John had written on April 2nd, the anniversary I'd missed.

Dear Lisa,

In normal times, today, our thirteenth anniversary, would have been a normal workday for me. I would have awoken at 4:45 a.m., gotten dressed, and left for work as you slept. As I went about my busy day, I may have called you midmorning to wish you Happy Anniversary, and planned a dinner for the night. I would have arrived with an anniversary card, a feeble attempt at professing my love for you, that I'd purchased on the way home. Over the years of our marriage you have begged, pleaded, and cried out for all of me, and for us to be bonded together in Christ. We both know I have fallen short, and for this I cry out for your forgiveness.

Through your sickness God has shown me what you and others have been trying to show me for years: that in you I have everything I could ever hope for, that you are a precious gift from God that I need to love and appreciate every day. I know now that I can skip the anniversary card and the dinners. All you really want from me is me. So today on our thirteenth anniversary I want to simply say that you are the most important person in my life, that I thank God for you, and I love you very much.

Happy Anniversary, John

When I'd read everything, I told John that from then on I wanted to write the journal entries myself. I had been stunned by the support, prayers, and encouragement my family had gotten, and wanted to acknowledge everything. "I can see that this was harder on you guys than on me," I told him.

The first words I typed were, "It's me..."

I wanted readers to know that I had once again become a thinking, feeling human being who needed help. I wanted people to visit me and to understand that just because I was awake and in therapy didn't mean I was well. Weak and scared was more like it. The first time I tried to walk I could only get as far as ten floor tiles before I was completely exhausted. My mom and dad stood there watching and crying. Afterward my mom said, "I don't know if I'm happier about you walking this time or when you were a baby!" I vowed to get stronger as fast as I could.

My health crisis has changed both John's and my perspective about what's important in life and what is not. So many of us let the little stuff grow out of proportion. We take relationships for granted because we think they're going to be here tomorrow, when they may not be. Why spend a lot of time bickering and arguing about little things when we could cherish that we have each other still? I used to complain all the time about going to the grocery store and doing the laundry, but when I finally came home after fifty-two days in the ICU, and I could no longer cook for myself or anyone, or do the laundry, I missed it. Now it's nice to do laundry, simply because I can.

Although we never expected that I would get seriously ill, John and I had talked about what would happen if I did. Could he really be there for me—and me for him—in a tragic circumstance? My children weren't his children, and I knew that he sometimes felt like an outsider. But would he act like one? Clearly not. We passed the test. My illness was a gift, a bonding experience for John and my children. I believe God put me to sleep so He could ensure that. My kids now look to John for advice, direction, and emotional support.

Those were my worries. Besides losing me, John had worried that I might not remember him when I woke up. He definitely didn't want me to see my ex-husband first, because what if I thought I was still married to him? I laugh now, but he was terrified.

John kept a personal journal while I was in the hospital, and when I came home, we read it together. He wrote about emotional moments that he didn't share on CaringBridge, like when I opened my eyes and smiled in recognition that first time. He said his heart warmed in a way it hadn't for a long time. He wrote about being grateful, about being at the hospital every day, on his knees, begging God, "Give me some more time, please! I'm not ready for this to be over." It was horrible for him.

His prayers had been granted. I'd come home.

One doesn't recover quickly from a ruptured aneurysm. I drive now, but for eight months the state took away my driver's license. At first I couldn't cook, but when I could, I had another challenge: to go grocery shopping. Hard to do if you can't drive the bags home. The first time I went to the grocery store with John, I was so tired that I would have sat on the floor in the middle of an aisle if it wouldn't have been so embarrassing. My solution was to shop for bits at a time, dragging a handcart. I walked there and back because I needed the exercise.

Eventually I could make it three and a half miles around a nearby lake, and that's when I asked the doctor to sign papers so I could get my license back. I had to go to a special DMV for medical conditions. I sat through an hour-and-a-half interview so they could make sure I was cognitively all there. After I passed the written test, I took the driving portion at a regular DMV. I was as nervous at forty-eight as I had been the first time I took the test at sixteen.

Once I was mobile, I drove to Mission Hospital every week. There I'd go to the family waiting room and introduce myself as a former patient. I'd let people tell me their stories if they wanted to. Sometimes they don't want to share; sometimes they're sitting on pins and needles wishing they had someone to talk with. I always asked if I could help in any way, and I'd bring CaringBridge brochures. Now there are stands with brochures all over the hospital, as well as four computer stations for doing updates.

I've visited the ambulance attendant several times to thank her for helping me. I go back to the fire station every year on the day, March 20th, to thank them. I go to the hospital. I deliver cupcakes and all kinds of gifts to let each department know how much I appreciate their help. I update them on what I've been doing over the year that I wouldn't have been able to do if I had passed away. The highlights: I have two grandchildren and a third one coming. I got to see my daughter get married. My son is getting married in September.

These are all big milestones that I would have missed if not for the help and prayers of so many.

> "If you want others to be happy, practice compassion. If you want to be happy, practice compassion."
>
> —*Dalai Lama*

ALEX PAUL

Strength to Live

ALEX: A few of my friends and I had miniature dirt bikes, and we'd stunt-ride them around parking lots or industrial park roads. The night of the accident, a friend and I went out and waited for the rest of our group to meet us. They came in three cars. In two were a couple of kids who I knew very well. Driving the third car was a kid I had just met the night before. As he pulled up, he decided to show off, so he zoomed past the two cars in front of him and went around a roundabout in the wrong direction.

I was riding my bike in the correct direction.

Neither of us had time to react. Both of us were going about forty miles an hour, and it was a head-on collision.

I went up over the hood, into the windshield. My legs hit the top front of the hood, denting in the hood about six inches. That flipped me forward and my head hit the windshield, on the driver's side, shattering the glass. Then the rest of my body folded around the side of the car, at which point my neck broke.

The driver was uninsured. His pregnant girlfriend was in the car. He had an unsecured toddler in the backseat. None of them were injured.

After the accident my friend ran over and found me in the grass on the side of the road. The kid that hit me got out of his car, ran over, and reached for me, but my friend grabbed him and threw him back because he knew that I shouldn't be touched. They called 911. Later, the EMTs said that when they held my head, my neck felt like Jell-O. There was nothing there.

My shoes were found forty feet away. A bracelet on my wrist was gone. The bike's metal frame was mangled, and the rest of it had just about disintegrated. The impact was so great the leather seat's seams burst and all the foam inside was forced out.

During surgery I slipped out of anesthesia. I was on a table, looked up, and saw a guy with a hammer. I had no idea what was going on. I said, "Why are you doing this?" Whether I actually said the words aloud or just thought them, I'm not sure. Then I guess I slipped under again. I found out later that the guy with the hammer was there when they were fixing my broken femur. They had to put an external cage around my leg to hold it in the proper position.

ANDY: I was at work when my wife, Pris, called around 7:00 p.m. I don't think I have ever traveled faster from North Berwick to Biddeford—twenty-three miles in twenty minutes. But as I left the turnpike, Pris called and said to forget about Biddeford. Alex had been sent to Maine Medical Center in Portland. That meant bad news.

At MMC I met Pris at the front desk. The receptionist was confused about who we were there for. Then, in a low voice, she told a volunteer, "Take them to family room three." My blood turned to ice.

It seemed an eternity before a physician came to brief us on Alex's status. His first words were, "Your son is a very sick young man...." After the rundown—fracture of the right patella, open fracture of the left femur, fractures of the cervical spine at C3, C4, and C5, possible other fractures that weren't yet detectable—we said, "We have a daughter in Connecticut. Should she be here?" The doctor said, "If it were my daughter, I'd want her here."

Alex had emergency surgery to clean and stabilize the open fracture that night. Early the following day, he had surgery to repair the damage to his right kneecap, left femur, and cervical spine. That took four and a half hours and was successful. The big question mark was what, if any, damage had been done to Alex's spine and what were the prospects for recovery. That's where the ambiguity began.

Pris asked the neurosurgeon if he could tell us with any certainty whether Alex would ever walk again, but he said that only time would tell.

Between surgeries, I went home to shower and change. There I found a pair of Alex's shoes by the back door. I carried them upstairs to his room and cried because I realized he'd probably never need them again.

PRIS: I didn't allow crying in the hospital room. Alex needed to be surrounded with strength. That night, Alex's girlfriend, Marina, met me in the parking lot. I was crying. She was upset. I said, "We're going in and we're not going to cry because he can probably hear us." Instead we talked to him and told him we loved him. But I have shed many, many, many tears.

Later, Alex asked a couple times, "Why can't I feel my legs?" We told him he'd had major surgery and to give it some time. Then, before any of us really wanted to admit it, he said, "Sell my car. I won't be driving my car." But I told him it was too early for that.

ALEX: When I first realized that I was paralyzed, I didn't take it as hard as people expected me to. I've thought about it since, and the fact is that I wasn't angry and I wasn't sad, and honestly I don't really know why. It just kind of hit me as, *Okay, this is something for me to work toward now. Moving. Walking. It's just another life battle that I'll have to deal with.* That's me. Whatever has come my way I deal with as it is. I can't focus on why it happened. I have to ask, What's next?

ANDY: Alex told me that he felt like he was trapped in a very tight suit of body armor. Afterward I lay awake wondering what it must be like to be alert and aware but a prisoner in an immobile body. I could not imagine. I wondered what his future would be like. Endless days of consciousness without stimulation? What kind of existence is that? I didn't want my thoughts to go there, but it was hard to stop, because we never know what the future holds. I knew we'd find out eventually, when he got out of the ICU and we found a rehabilitation facility. His ability to function might improve. Or it might already be as good as it would ever get.

ALEX: That entire month in the ICU was pretty much a blur. I was in and out of consciousness, drugged up. But I do know this: JP, the friend I'd been with the night of the accident, did not miss visiting for a single day. He'd come after work and both days on the weekend. That was awesome. And my girlfriend, Marina, was always there, too.

MARINA: I was only nineteen. I'd never had to deal with anything like Alex's situation. People ask how I did it and I just don't know. Day by day, I guess, because I couldn't look into the future, and there was no point in looking backward and being mad about something that had already happened.

ALEX: The one person I never saw and still haven't heard from is the guy who hit me. If he walked in the room now, the only thing I'd ask is how he deals with what happened. I don't understand how he can live with knowing what happened without ever wanting to try and settle the situation, without even talking about it. He changed my life. How can he sleep at night?

PRIS: If he walked in now, I couldn't say anything. But I'd let him take a good long look around, absorb, and see what goes on here.

ANDY: Alex's initial neuro exam showed a lack of sensation below the level of his chest and from his elbows down. He could move his shoulders, upper arms, and bend his elbows, but that was it. Since the level of the spinal cord injury corresponded with the level of the lowest fracture (C5), the muscles that control his breathing, his diaphragm, and chest-wall muscles were impacted, and he was totally dependent on a ventilator for breathing. The tube from the ventilator in his mouth made talking impossible until Alex had a tracheostomy, which involved cutting a hole at the base of his throat, just above his breastbone, to insert and anchor his breathing tube. Communication improved, but I could have used a course in lip reading. At one point Alex struggled mightily to get us to "suction" his mouth. We thought he was telling us to "suck sh*t."

Our goal was to get Alex into a spinal cord injury (SCI) rehabilitation program, but he had to deal with other problems before that could happen. Alex had a collapsed lung and needed two bronchoscopies, which involves inserting a suction tube into his lung to remove normal lung secretions and, subsequently, rinsing the lung with water and suctioning that out. He had pneumonia, and an ileus (a GI obstruction). He took antibiotics for the pneumonia, had a nasogastric tube (NG) inserted up his nose and down into his intestine to address the ileus, and had a chest tube inserted to address the collapsed lung. He took narcotic pain meds and anxiety drugs.

Alex also had to be examined by a physiatrist—a rehab physician—in order to determine which facility would be best. The accepting facility wanted to know his status before deciding whether to accept him in their program. What he told us was essentially what we knew a week earlier: he had a spinal cord injury at the C5 level, and he was going nowhere until his blood pressure and heart rate were stabilized. Both declined when he was moved into a sitting position, and he was infection-and-sore free.

Within a couple of days of that exam, Alex got over his fever. The doctors put in a peripherally inserted central catheter (PICC) line to facilitate long-term infusions. IVs inserted into arms or hands really are not intended for long-term use; after a few days they become irritated and may be points of entry for infectious agents. The PICC allows long-term access to administer antibiotics or pain medications.

Alex continued to have physical therapy with the immediate goal of getting him into an upright position and to tolerate sitting. But Alex's heart rate and blood pressure fluctuated and he got dizzy. The doctors tried a drug to elevate his blood pressure, and he was able to sit up for almost ninety minutes. Another small and crucial victory. Once he could sit, we wheeled a laptop computer to his bedside and showed him his CaringBridge site. He enjoyed the photos and guest-book entries.

Then Alex had three good days in a row. The pneumonia was gone. The ileus, gone. Chest tube, gone. NG tube, gone. No pain meds. Blood pressure and heart rate stabilized. He could tolerate sitting upright for longer periods each day. He began to breathe on his own for longer each day. He went more than twenty-four hours without pain meds or complaining about pain.

And most encouraging, Pris was stroking his forearm and he said, "I feel that." He could also feel the sensation of light touch on his thumb and index finger: places where he'd felt no sensation before. We hoped that meant some healing. It might not, but it was a good moment.

At the end of each day during the weeks after the accident, Alex was always tired, and it was in those moments that I knew he was most vulnerable. While he had made great strides—fighting off problems, moving forward over the roughest terrain—in those moments Alex also realized what he had lost and the long and uncertain road to regaining his independence.

Each of us experienced our own moments of poignancy during the last few minutes of every visit. Life would be different for us all if not for the accident, but it still is life, and life is better than the alternative.

PRIS: The first few days after the accident the phones were blowing up with calls. Andy has a large family, who all wanted to know what had happened, and then we began hearing from people in the community, and realized that some of them had the details wrong. We decided to put all the facts in the same place, where the information would come from Andy and me, and you'd know you could depend on it. Period. End of discussion. The hospital told us about CaringBridge, and I remembered going there before. Posting in the journal became efficient, not to mention more than just writing. It was therapy.

ALEX: Even after all this time I have not gone back to read the journal. I guess I don't want to go back to that time. Not that I don't want to know how I was at that point, but how I was then doesn't matter to me anymore at all. I have to let it go. If something new happens and I'm able to do something else on my own, great, but again that's not what I want to focus on. I want to work toward something bigger and better. Going back to the journal would be focusing on how things used to be and not what will be. Also, I'd have to experience my parents' pain.

PRIS: He knows it's there. We read some of the guest-book entries to him until he got to the point of "Okay, that's enough." Alex doesn't show much emotion. That's part of who he is. I have to let it out, though. I cry and then feel better. He holds everything in. But maybe it's just because we're his parents. He's more open with Marina, which is fine. That's how it should be at his age. As long as Alex has an emotional outlet, I'm happy. But I confess there are times when, for my own emotional health, I'd love it if he would open up to us.

MARINA: My friends kept asking me if I was going to stay with Alex. I'd never thought about leaving. Alex asked, too, and then it was a big deal. I started crying, unfortunately, and I told him I was going to have to leave the room. I didn't want him to think that. I didn't want him to be afraid that one day I wouldn't be there. It hurt my feelings that he thought I would even consider leaving.

ALEX: I knew that I would never be the one to let go. Had it crossed my mind that she would end it with me? Absolutely. But I left it completely up to her. I wasn't going to end it just because I thought that's what she needed. I assumed that if she wanted or needed to go, she'd let me know on her own.

PRIS: While we were researching a rehabilitation facility for Alex, we heard the word *quadriplegic* for the first time. Twice, actually. We're not naive. We'd seen it on the paperwork that we had to fill out to gain conservatorship and guardianship over Alex, and the physician had filled out her portion. It still took my breath away. Before that, the doctor had not been willing to be definitive. I asked, "Are you saying he'll never walk again?" The doctor said, "Oh, no, no, no. We just don't know." I had completely tucked away that sliver of hope until the day I saw "quadriplegic" on paper. Then I couldn't get it out of my head, and I felt completely overwhelmed.

ANDY: We toured Spaulding Rehabilitation Hospital and Boston Medical Center. Both have model spinal cord injury rehabilitation programs; both have good points; and both could accept Alex immediately. A dilemma. An embarrassment of riches. Two world-class SCI programs practically in our backyard. But it wasn't our decision. Alex had to decide.

While we were in Boston, we heard that the physical therapist got Alex up in a wheelchair and took him on a tour. He left his room for the first time in three weeks (excluding trips to the OR). They wheeled him down to the lobby, and they took him outside in the courtyard for a few minutes. He loved it. Marina texted us a wonderful picture of him in his wheelchair, surrounded by friends, with the biggest smile on his face. It's the first time we'd seen him smile in weeks.

The doctors put a valve in his trachea that let him speak a little. He didn't like it, but Alex told us he was anxious to choose a rehab facility and asked us to "stop delaying." We agreed. It had become more and more obvious each day that Alex no longer required acute care and was ready to start the next phase of his recovery. He'd had no crises for a week, and his only remaining issues were relying on the ventilator (less and less) and needing to be repositioned every two hours. We notified the discharge coordinator that Alex would go to rehab at Boston Medical Center.

ANDY: As Alex worked to get off the ventilator in rehab, he sometimes had to cough, especially when they passed a tube down his tracheostomy to suction the secretions from his lungs. When he coughed, the effort caused the muscles in his arms to contract, bending his elbows and wrists so that his arms tucked in, wrists under his chin, and hands pointed down. After he finished, we'd have to straighten his arms out and place rolled facecloths in his hands so that his fingers didn't develop a permanent curl. But one day, after coughing, he was able to straighten his arms on his own, and he placed his own hands over the rolled facecloths. Not only that, he reached for and was able to place his hand on the TV remote. He was angry because he couldn't punch the buttons to change the channel, but still, it was a level of muscle control we had not seen, and it is just this kind of frustration that would drive him to achieve more control.

ALEX: Even before the accident I never wanted things to be done for me. I always tried to be as independent as possible. Needing help is still new to me and I have trouble dealing with that. Sometimes it makes me angry, but I used that energy to continue to work toward doing more and more on my own.

ANDY: A couple of weeks after Alex entered rehab, we got a call from his attending physician, to update us on Alex's status. Before Alex left the hospital, he'd been examined by a physiatrist. The exam was incomplete, but the assumption was that Alex's injury was a "complete" spinal cord injury, no sensation and no function below the level of his injury. Since transferring to Boston Medical Center, his assessment had been completed. The doctor was happy to inform us, and we were happy to hear, that Alex's injury was "incomplete." Spinal cord injuries are classified as A, B, C, D, or E, with A being a complete injury, E being a completely normal spinal cord. We had thought Alex's injury was an A, but it's a C. This didn't mean Alex had gotten better since transferring to rehab, it just meant that he had the potential of regaining some function that we otherwise would not have expected. The doctor said that the letter designation could change in either direction but that with rehabilitation any movement is generally in the direction of improved function. Factors that influence positive change include the severity of the injury, how quickly sensation returns, age (younger is better), condition, and motivation.

None of this was a guarantee that Alex would get any better, but he had a lot of factors in his favor. We were also told that the greatest factor in overall recovery is time, meaning that we wouldn't know the final outcome for Alex soon. Spinal cord injuries take a long time to reach maximum improvement. Still, the doctor left us guardedly optimistic about Alex's prospects. He had more tools in his toolbox—and a lot of work still ahead.

PRIS: Sometimes Alex would surprise us by being able to move in ways he hadn't before. Or he could feel something.

MARINA: I was massaging Alex's left hand and suddenly he said, "I feel that!" He looked shocked. He could feel my touch on the middle and ring fingers.

ANDY: It's a huge leap from feeling sensation to actually making his fingers move at will. But, all forward progress was good news.

One day, I got a text message from Marina: "Alex's trach is out, and he moved his toes on both feet!"

During that week, Alex drove a powered wheelchair on his own (Monday); had his tracheostomy tube removed and began breathing without assistance and without problems (Tuesday); moved his toes on each of his feet (Tuesday); was cleared to eat anything he wanted (Tuesday); fed himself (Tuesday); had his first session on the Electric Stimulation Cycle, and said his legs felt tired (Thursday); posted a message to his girlfriend's Facebook page without assistance (Thursday); and powered himself down the halls of Boston Medical Center in a manual wheelchair (Friday).

His physical therapist told him his was the fastest wean from a ventilator they had seen. He also said he was stunned that Alex didn't require assistance from a sling when he fed himself.

When Alex was first injured and we started our education about spinal cord injury, I prayed that one day he would attain the level of function he had at that moment attained. Shame on me for having had such low expectations! He'd attained so much thanks to his own will and determination to overcome obstacles, and a lot of faith, support, and prayer from family, friends, neighbors, and his extended community.

As time went by, Alex surprised us with his ability to do even more. At one point he mentioned matter-of-factly that he had sensation all the way down to his fingertips in both hands. He woke up one morning with a pain in his left foot. His skin produced goose bumps during a cool bath. He could twitch his finger and move his thumb.

We had no doubt that he had a tough road ahead. His diagnosis was, after all, quadriplegia. But quadriplegia simply means impairment in all four extremities, and there are different levels of impairment. Some quadriplegics function at very high levels. We learned that independence is possible. Even driving a motor vehicle is possible. When we cautioned Alex—who once wanted us to sell his car—that he couldn't consider driving for at least a year, he said, "I'm not going to be in this chair forever. In a year I'll be walking." If it is at all physically possible, I have no doubt that Alex will achieve his goal.

ALEX: I don't see myself as a quadriplegic. That's not me at all. That's not how I think my friends relate to me, either. At first I was worried that people would see me that way, but my experience is that they see me as the exact same person I was before. I'm not "the kid in the wheelchair." I'm Alex. What's tough for me is not being able to physically help others.

I was an auto mechanic for years, and my friends and I spent our spare time working on our vehicles. We all like to tinker, and I'd help out a lot whenever they had any issues. People still come to me with questions, and now it's hard not to be able to actually show them what to do. But I don't shy away from it, either. I will still walk them through the process verbally, as much as I can. My friends still listen to me. They know the knowledge is still there even if my body won't cooperate. Marina just changed out a radio in my truck. I assumed it was something she couldn't do, but she said, "Walk me through it, and I'll do it." So I sat in the truck and walked her through, step by step, and she did it without any issues at all.

My attitude is not to underestimate myself. You might think that you can't handle something emotionally or physically, but you're a lot stronger than you think you are. You'll just never know that strength until you need it. Just because you don't use it or because you don't recognize it doesn't mean that you don't have it.

ANDY: About two years ago, when Alex was an able-bodied mechanic working at Neil's Motors, he got himself a 1991 Chevrolet Fleetside short-box pickup truck. He spent a lot of time and money building the truck of his dreams. He took it to car shows and won trophies. Then he got the itch for a fast motorcycle. Being short on cash, he traded his dream truck for a Yamaha R6. That bike was a rocket!

We all know what's said about the grass always being greener. Before long he began to miss his truck, but his truck was no longer his. So he found another '91 short-box. The body was sound, but it needed paint, and the gutted cabin needed to be restored. Alex bought a new motor but hadn't installed it. And then the accident happened.

Last summer one of Alex's friends told him they saw his truck on Craigslist. Alex looked like a young puppy in love. Using a modest return on his income taxes plus what he was able to sell his project truck for, he was able to buy back his baby.

He couldn't wait to get in it. Since he had tinkered with the truck's suspension to bring the entire body closer to the ground—that's called "lowering it"—getting him into it was no problem at all. Someday, when he is able to drive, it will be easier for him to transfer into this vehicle than into most others.

Alex has come a long way. He still has problems—bladder infections, some surgery on a kneecap, blood pressure fluctuating and inhibiting rehab. But one day last summer Alex told us that his butt felt all "pins and needles," the feeling you get when you sit in one spot too long. He also said he could feel that his knees were bent, and he could feel the footplate of his wheelchair under his feet. He has felt each of these things in the past, but not so persistently. Unfortunately, he felt none of it the next day. Still... first comes feeling, then comes function.

PRIS: The strength of family and friends and community really helped us get through this initial ordeal. I don't know that we would have been able to do as much as we have without that support. People left us food to eat. My brother took care of the leaves. The neighbor across the street took care of snowblowing the yard in the wintertime. It's all of those little things together that helped us get through this. I don't think we realized the big community we had behind us. None of us really did. The day after Alex came home, some people formed a fund-raising committee and held a dance at a local club. The club holds 450 people. Andy and I don't even know that many people.

Alex was determined to go to the dance. We pulled into the parking lot, and the place was packed. That just blew us away.

When Alex was transferred to Boston for rehab, we traveled there every weekend. While we were away, one of Andy's co-workers took it upon himself to put up a ramp at the house. We got pictures of the work in progress and it included people we didn't even know.

Why do people do that? It still has me scratching my head. People say, "You would do the same thing in return." For family? Absolutely. For friends? Absolutely. But for a total stranger? Before the accident, I don't know that I would have. Now I would.

Part of what kept us going, even though some days were very dark, was the simple fact that we had Alex. We were fortunate not to lose him completely. There are still days when I cry. We all do. But this is what our normal life is now, so we either move forward or spend the rest of our lives in the dark. What I've learned is to take it one day at a time. I can't look at the whole picture because it's too overwhelming. But every day that we get through is another milestone.

Yesterday I went to the mall with Alex for the first time. I watched shoppers watching him and Marina. I couldn't help but wonder what was going through their minds. I hoped they didn't feel sorry for him, because there's nothing to feel sorry about. He's fortunate to have the girlfriend that he has and the friends that he has, and the family he has. His friends come to get him, and off they go together. Alex's life is different, but it's still relatively full.

ALEX: The next thing for me is starting quadriplegic rugby. I was always an active kid, always trying to do anything to take up my day rather than sit around. Quad rugby will enable me to be the same active person that I was before.

The first time that I met the rugby team, they asked what happened and when it happened. I told them I was in an accident with a car while I was riding my dirt bike, and that was it. We moved on quickly.

Being around those guys is very comforting. We're all in the same situation, so I can ask them about anything I want to know. There's no judgment. My physical and occupational therapists can explain how to do something or tell me to try something a certain way all they want. But when it comes down to it, they can't know exactly what it's like to be me. To be able to talk to guys who are living it is far better. For instance, I had some mobility questions. What driving adaptations do they use? What activities do they participate in? Some guys on the rugby team still snowmobile. To talk to them about how they do it is to hear that everything is possible, no matter what. Quads just do it a little differently. Will it be just as easy? No. But it is possible.

ANDY: Alex suggested that everyone in the family get a tattoo to demonstrate our solidarity in a visible way. It would be a simple slogan that described his will throughout the ordeal: "Strength to Live." We started by making wristbands, but when the time comes, I'm in.

Five Ways to Help a Family during a Health Crisis

1. Depending on the time of year, mow the lawn, rake the leaves, or shovel the snow. The advantage with this kind of gift is that you don't necessarily have to get permission—show up with your own tools and get to work!

2. Drive children to and from school and to and from after school activities. Offer to host them after school to do homework and hang out with your own kids.

3. Walk the family dog.

4. Find out about any food allergies before delivering casseroles, and then plan to divvy up the dish into single-serving portions that can be frozen. Always include reheating instructions on the containers. Use disposable containers whenever possible.

5. Consider foods that don't need to be refrigerated and don't involve a lot of prep work. A refrigerator can fill up pretty fast if everyone starts dropping off casseroles. Fresh fruits and bakery breads and pastries are welcome alternatives.

BREE ANDERSON

It's All about the Moments

My husband, Scott, and I were high school sweethearts in Ghent, Minnesota, a town even smaller than Minneota, where we live now and where there are only fourteen hundred people. We got married after college, the first among our siblings, and tried to get pregnant right away, because we knew it was going to be hard. I'd always had problems with my periods, and Scott and I talked about my fertility problems many times before we got married.

We found a reproductive endocrinologist at Sanford Medical Center in Sioux Falls, South Dakota, and we tried every available drug—with no success. Then we tried artificial insemination eleven different times. You cycle, you're not pregnant, you do an insemination. You cycle, you're not pregnant, you do an insemination. Repeat eleven times. Scott spent a lot of time in the collection room doing what he had to do.

A lot of my friends just got pregnant without hardly trying: "Hey, let's have sex and make a baby. Oh look, I'm pregnant!" It didn't piss me off. We always knew it would be a challenge for us. I was too busy with our own process and how it was affecting us as a couple, and me as a woman.

We had one option left: in vitro fertilization, IVF. We decided to try it one or two times, and if it didn't work, we'd attempt an international adoption. I knew someone who had adopted from Russia, which was faster than adopting an American baby, and it appealed to me. It didn't matter to us where the baby came from or what it looked like. I just wanted a baby to love. We were fully ready.

The IVF process was intense. I gave myself shots in the stomach three times a day. After the embryos were transplanted, Scott gave me intramuscular shots twice a day in addition to the stomach shots I continued to give myself. One day I walked out of the pharmacy with a cooler full of $10,000 worth of fertility drugs. Thank God my husband has amazing insurance.

Shortly after the embryo transplant I started feeling very weird. My body never thought I should be pregnant, and now it was producing too much of the pregnancy hormone HCG. I had gone into ovarian hyperstimulation, which produced a fluid buildup around my lungs and in my upper abdomen. I lost about a third of my lung function and I could barely breathe. I was in the hospital for nine days.

While I was there, the reproductive endocrinologist came to my room and said, "I have something amazing to tell you. You're pregnant."

"Thank God," I said. "I was hoping I wasn't this sick in the hospital for nothing."

Then he added, "I think you're going to have twins."

I didn't know if I should be excited. It was so soon, much sooner than anyone usually finds out she's pregnant with an IVF process. Scott and I were cautious and didn't tell anyone because, frankly, everybody and their brother in Minneota already knew that I'd had two embryos implanted and was just waiting. You talk about it at the local restaurant, somebody hears you, and then everybody knows.

A couple of weeks after I came out of the hospital, we shared the news with our families that we were officially nine weeks pregnant, but we thought it was too early to tell them we were having twins. In anticipation, we had asked the ultrasound technician to isolate one of the babies and take that picture so we could show it around. We said, "I guess the second embryo didn't attach, but that's okay. We're going to have one happy, healthy baby!"

It was kind of anticlimactic. Our families said, "Oh, that's really good, dear. We were hoping one of the embryos would stick."

Eventually we had to tell everyone we were having twins. We went with Scott's parents and grandmother, and my parents and grandparents to CJ's, a local restaurant. I made gift packages for everybody with twin packs of whatever I could find, things like Doublemint gum and Act II popcorn. We're all big Minnesota Twins fans, so at the bottom of the bag, in case they hadn't figured it out yet, was a Twins logo that I had edited to read *Minneota* Twins. Scott's mom, Anita, saw the Doublemint and the popcorn and in two seconds said, "You're having twins!" My mom hadn't caught on even a little bit. She hadn't heard what Anita said and was still looking in the bag. I said, "Mom, did you hear?" She said, "No, what?" Anita looked at her, started crying, and said, "We're going to have twin grandbabies!"

That's what I wanted, that excitement and surprise!

Being pregnant was the most amazing thing in the world. I didn't think I'd ever get to do it, and when I did, there were two.

I felt so good. I felt like I had a purpose. With twins you start showing very early, so I was in maternity clothes by about sixteen weeks. And we learned we were having boys.

When you're having a baby, twenty-four weeks is the magic number. If, by the most horrible circumstances, you have to deliver a baby at twenty-four weeks, it will have at least a tiny shot at life. Twenty-three weeks and six days was a Friday. I was working as a substitute schoolteacher and was subbing in the band room that day. I felt very strange. By the third or fourth hour I had to tell the new class coming in that they couldn't play the drums because it was really bothering me. I thought I was having contractions.

The next day was a Saturday. Twenty-four weeks. Sixteen more weeks to go. *We can do this,* I thought. *And if something happens, at least I know my babies might live, but that's not going to happen to me. We're going to make it.* But I was restless. My mom noticed that I was fidgety, moving my hips and trying to get comfortable at the kitchen table.

Sunday night I woke up wet. I went into the bathroom and the fluid was clear and sticky. I freaked out. I woke up my husband. We called the emergency people at Sanford Medical Center, two hours away in Sioux Falls, South Dakota, who woke up my doctor. He told us to get to the hospital as soon as possible. We knew we could be on the road for a half hour already before an ambulance arrived, so we got in the car.

Scott drove ninety-five miles an hour at least. We prayed that we'd get pulled over so the police could escort us and we could get to the hospital safely going that fast. We didn't see one cop.

At the hospital they took me to the high-risk obstetrics area. I felt like I was in the middle of a *CSI* episode. Technicians and doctors came in with what looked like a big tackle box, and used the devices inside to test whether I was in labor and whether the liquid was amniotic fluid. They actually used a swab that turns color if there is blood present, just like they use on *CSI*. The swab changed color. The fluid was definitely amniotic.

An ultrasound revealed that I had a pinhole leak in Baby A's amniotic sac. The nurses comforted me. They said, "Pinhole leaks happen all the time. You're going to be here until you deliver, but that could be for a long time and you could deliver big babies." The neonatologist came in to remind us that I was not very far along in my pregnancy and that the babies would be very sick if they were born right now. To prevent that, I needed to do everything I was told to do.

Soon they moved me to a mommy-to-be room in a wing with people who were all like me: absolutely terrified of what was going to happen and when it was going to happen. The nurses were very caring and kept us calm.

I wasn't having any contractions and I wasn't dilated, but a pinhole leak can turn into a full rupture, so you have to remain on bed rest. I could get up maybe once a day to go to the bathroom and take a shower, but the rest of the time I would use a bedpan.

Monday was a fairly quiet day. Our parents all came to visit. Monday night, my father-in-law helped me out of bed for my daily trip to the bathroom. But when I stood up, I had a full rupture—all over his feet. I don't think he'll ever forget it, and I'll surely never forget the look on his face.

Scott ran out to tell the nurses what had happened. Minutes later, my favorite friend, the ultrasound machine, arrived again to see how much amniotic fluid was left. Baby A's amniotic sac was maybe half empty, but a mother's body keeps producing more, so that was okay. I just had to sit very, very still, almost flat or even inverted, so the fluid wouldn't continue to leak. I couldn't get out of bed even once now, but I was willing to be stuck.

On Tuesday, at about 3:30 in the morning, I told Scott I really had to poop, and I pleaded with him to get me out of bed. He helped me to the toilet but nothing happened. I got back in bed, and Scott went out to tell the nurses. They weren't too worried about it; they assumed I was constipated. About 5:30 a.m. I had the same feeling. Scott took me to the bathroom again and then went to get the nurses while I sat on the toilet. I didn't have any idea I was in labor—no clue—until it started to hurt really, really, *really* badly. The pain was insane.

My memories of what followed are so vivid that I start crying just thinking about them, even though they happened more than five years ago.

The nurses got me off the toilet and back in bed and aimed a huge fluorescent light between my legs to look inside. A nurse looked up at me and said, "I feel parts."

I said, "What parts?"

"His feet."

"Where are they?"

"They're in your vagina."

"I don't know what that means."

"That means that we have to have these babies right now."

They immediately started prepping me for a C-section. I panicked. "We can't do this," I said.

"It's not time," Scott said.

"It's only twenty-four weeks and three days. It's way too early," I said as they wheeled me to the operating room. "We're going to...I don't want to have dead babies."

In the operating room, about two dozen medical personnel had assembled to deliver two babies. The perinatologist checked me and said, "This baby is too far down. I can't push him back up for the C-section. You have to deliver him this way."

"My Lamaze classes aren't for two weeks," I told a nurse. "I don't know what to do."

She gave me a little smile and said, "I'll tell you what to do, and I know you can do it." Her voice was so calm. I focused on her voice, and all the people in the room disappeared. The only people I saw were the perinatologist between my knees, the nurse, and my husband.

The doctor said, "This is going to be hard because you aren't dilated all the way and your body doesn't have anything to contract against because the babies are so little. You have to do this and you have to do it right now. If you don't, he will die." I gave him a knowing if frantic nod. The nurse told me what to do and I pushed.

The baby came out feetfirst, and his head got stuck for a moment. He was too little to cry. The neonatologist didn't think she was going to be able to save him, that he would just slip away, but she tried with whatever she could. I think I remember seeing a little glimpse of his toes when she was trying to intubate him, and I remember her grabbing the tube, but I couldn't see all of him. Then they took him away. There was nothing I could do. I just lay there on the table. It was 6:05 a.m.

I got a magnesium sulfate drip to slow the labor for the next baby. No one really expected it to work in my situation, but they hoped, so they tried. By the time the perinatologist looked between my legs again, my cervix was completely closed. My contractions had stopped. No second baby would be born that day.

Scott and I went back to my room, turned off the phone, and shut the shades. We asked for a CD player and some soft music so we could try to calm down. We had already decided on the babies' names: Carter Douglas and Logan Darrell, after their grandpas. Douglas is my stepdad's name and Darrell is Scott's dad's name. We named the new baby Carter. The doctor came in a while later and said, "There's no sign that you're going to be having a second baby anytime soon. We'll keep you on the monitor and keep you posted on how Carter is doing."

I called my mom at work and said, "Are you sitting down?"

"Oh my God," she gasped. "What happened?"

I said, "Go get Laurie, and then sit down."

She got her friend Laurie.

"Carter Douglas was born at six-oh-five," I said. "He weighs one pound five ounces. His head is smaller than a baseball, and he's only twelve and a half inches long."

"And?"

"And he's stable right now."

"What about…?"

"Logan Darrell has not been born yet."

"What?!"

"Logan is still inside of me and there is no sign of him coming out today."

When my mom stopped crying, she asked if we wanted her to come. I said we were fine, but she insisted. I was thinking that I was okay and I was stable. I wasn't thinking that she might want to see her grandson before he died.

We had Carter baptized as soon as the family arrived. I couldn't get out of bed, so they wheeled me and the bed into the NICU for the ceremony. It was a brand-new NICU, where every baby has his own room, almost like in a hotel. It was so nice. I felt my stomach and thought, *Why couldn't I have kept him inside me for just a little bit longer? Why does the one in here get to be happy while the one out there is almost dying in a struggle to live?*

We found out later that this sort of thing normally happens much earlier in the pregnancy and that the first baby born is the "sacrifice twin." The baby born first usually has an infection or has something wrong to the point where the mother's body thinks that one baby needs to be put out so the other baby can live.

But Logan, who was still inside of me, had his struggles too. I was constantly monitored, and when I started having contractions, his heart rate would drop and then pop back up. After a couple of days of this, he began having a harder time recovering, so the nurses started giving me oxygen and positioning me on my left side to increase the blood flow to him.

One morning the perinatologist said, "I don't want to say what's right and wrong here, because this is a situation I've never been in before, but I don't want this birth to be an emergency like it was with Carter. You have a choice to make. We're monitoring you every minute and can maybe sense when the emergency is coming. But we don't know how long this will take. And if the contractions get any bigger, he could die in the womb before he is born."

So at 10:00 in the morning, on the fifth of December, we decided to let the doctors deliver Baby B.

Logan cried when he was born, and he was pink, not purple. He was two weeks older than Carter in the womb, and two weeks younger outside of it. When Carter was born, I could see through his skin. His eyelids were fused and he looked like a naked baby bird. He was kind of scary to look at. Logan was not. Logan wasn't quite two pounds, but he looked like a baby. When he was delivered, the nurses brought him right to my face so I could give him a kiss, and then they whisked him away to intubate him.

Logan was also sick, but he was a picture-perfect twenty-six-weeker. He gained weight and pulled through and did fine. But he's a miracle too. Twenty-six weeks and born weighing less than two pounds is so scary.

———————

Scott had been vigilant in the NICU after Carter was born, because I couldn't get out of bed. Each baby in the NICU had his own nurse. Scott and Carter's nurse got to talking and she told him about CaringBridge. Scott told me, "We can put pictures up and tell people how Carter is doing every day. Do you want to do that?" I said, "Of course I do." Good thing, because he had already set it up.

The first thing I'd look at when I opened our site was the ticker that counted visitors. That was the first sign to me that the news was getting out, that people were getting updates straight from us, and that so many people cared to check in and see how our babies were doing. The messages that people left were so encouraging and so heartfelt. The NICU is a very lonely place, and especially after Logan was born, I didn't leave for weeks and weeks at a time. I had only doctors and nurses to talk to. CaringBridge was the friend that I could turn to and where I could talk to other people, and in a matter of a few hours they would talk back.

Sometimes I look back at the journal entries and I'm amazed at what I wrote. On certain days Carter had less than 5 percent chance of surviving, yet there I was, writing in a very upbeat manner. I was much more scared than I seemed, but I didn't want to frighten readers. I didn't lie about anything, but I kept some of the specifics to myself.

When Carter was about four weeks old, they noticed a very large dark spot on his abdomen. They put in a drainage tube and found that it was stool. He was transferred to Minneapolis and they took out 70 percent of his small intestine. The surgeon said, "I think he has plenty left, but you'll have to keep monitoring him." When Carter got healthy enough—and by "healthy" I mean not trying to die—the gastroenterologist told me that 30 percent is right at the cusp of whether you will have short bowel syndrome or you will thrive.

About a month later, I was drinking coffee in the hospital cafeteria with my cell phone turned off. Finally I happened to look down at the phone and saw that I had eleven missed calls. I rushed up to the NICU and the nurses were waiting for me at the door. They said, "Carter is really sick and we don't know what's wrong, but he has air in his liver and we think it's necrotizing enterocolitis." We went to Minneapolis a second time.

Carter had an ileostomy and then got an infection. His chances of survival were extremely thin. Scott and I planned his funeral. We knew that we were going to get the call to come and hold him before he died. We just knew it.

The call never came.

In the Minneapolis NICU the next morning, the doctor said, "We don't know what happened. We don't know what we did. We didn't really do anything. But the air in his liver is gone. Carter is going to be fine." There was no reason for the necrotizing enterocolitis to all of a sudden be gone, but it was.

When you're in any situation that is stressful, scary, and life-threatening, you can't do days. You can't do hours. You can't do minutes. Those are specific quantities. It's really all about the moments. If Logan is having a good moment *right now*, I don't care how long that moment lasts. Whether it is thirty seconds or three hours, I don't care. I just know that that moment is fantastic. Carter's moments were shorter. He was so sick that it was about how many moments we felt good about *that day*. I didn't like thinking about numbers—less than 5 percent, less than 10 percent, only twenty-four weeks. I wanted to think about Carter getting better. And if right then, in the moment his oxygen saturation and his blood pressure were good and he did not have a fever, that was a good moment.

I have flashbacks to that time every single day. A certain noise will sound like one of the monitor alarms. Something will smell like a medicine they were given or a plastic bag that a medicine was hung in. The flashbacks would have been traumatic if one of the boys hadn't made it.

My "sacrifice twin" lived. Today Carter is six years old and a daily reminder that anything can happen. I have no idea what God's vision is for Carter, but I know it's something good, because he's still here, and he's so normal that people who don't know our story would never believe what he's been through.

I look at everything in life differently now, not just the kids. Every single thing that I encounter every day I appreciate more because of that journey that we went through with Carter and Logan.

You can limit access to your CaringBridge site, but we kept ours open for everyone to read and post. People from all over, people who wrote, "You don't know me, but...," yet had somehow heard of us from friends or relatives, followed the story because they wanted to pray for us and support us. Their innate ability and desire to care about fellow humans on a level like that was so comforting. I didn't mind that strangers read our website. If they cared enough to read it, then I knew that they cared how Carter and Logan were doing.

We got help in the mail all the time. People would write and say they knew that Scott was driving a lot, going to work during the day and then to the hospital to see the boys, so "Here's some gas money." There was nothing else they could do except pray and help us out a little bit like that. It was heartwarmingly huge.

The first Christmas after Carter and Logan were home, a handwritten letter came with the return address scratched off. All that remained was a city and a state. The letter said, "We heard about your story from a friend and we've followed you on CaringBridge for the past year and a half. We want you to know that we care about you and that we prayed for you every day, even though we didn't know you. Merry Christmas." Inside was $500. We never found out who sent it. Humanity is amazing.

By the way, both Carter and Logan lost a tooth today.

> "None of us knows what might happen even the next minute, yet still we go forward. Because we trust. Because we have faith."
> —*Paulo Coelho*, Brida

TRACI CLANCY

Making Cancer a Gift

I'd had a lump in my right breast for a couple of years, but every time I had my annual mammogram, they'd say, "It's just fibrocystic stuff. You're fine. Cut down on your caffeine." Then I went on a diet, lost weight, and could really feel the lump. When I told my sister that sometimes the lump would throb, she insisted I go back to the doctor. The doctor wanted to schedule a mammogram in about a month, but when I said, "Well, it's kind of hurting," the office fit me in the next day.

The new test had surprising results: nothing showed up on my right breast, but they found a little spot in my left breast. They immediately sent me down the hall for an ultrasound that confirmed the spot. I had a biopsy right away on both breasts. The results would take two days.

No one likes uncertainty, but I was used to it. I grew up as a navy brat. I was born in California, moved to—among other places—the northern tip of Honshu Island in Japan for four years when I was ten, and had friends all over the world.

When my father retired to Florida, I worked my way through college in Pensacola forty hours a week in a Baskin-Robbins at Elgin Air Force Base. I met a lot of Naval Aviators, nice young college graduates who, when they saw me and my friends from work, would say, "Oh, it's our ice-cream girls!" My life was right out of *An Officer and a Gentleman*.

My husband, John, had been to the Air Force Academy before coming to Elgin. He tells everybody that by marrying me he saved me from the navy guys. We soon had our first son, Kevin, then Patrick, and I quit working to become a stay-at-home mom for eight years. On the side, I got involved in shooting school pictures. I had just started a job as a sales rep when I was waiting for the biopsy results.

My colleagues at work kept me busy so I wouldn't worry, and mostly I didn't. But every once in a while a big fear would fill the pit of my stomach: *Holy crap, what if this is really cancer?* But I was young. I was healthy, five-eight and 160 pounds. My husband, who'd spent lots of time researching breast cancer online, was the terrified one. I stayed away from the computer, knowing I'd just imagine I had whatever symptoms or diseases I read about.

After a week John and I went to the hospital to meet with the radiologist and get the test results. "It's probably no big deal," I assured a friend with whom I was supposed to shoot pictures that evening at the school dance. "I'll be back in plenty of time."

John and I tried to stay positive, even cracking up at the

hospital when we heard the PA system paging "Doctor Beaver, extension four-twenty-three." Had to be an ob-gyn, right? We were still relaxed in the waiting room because I'd heard that if the lump hurts, it's probably not cancer, and if it's on both sides, it's probably not cancer. I was still thinking, *I do not have this. There's no way*, as we were ushered into the doctor's office.

I don't remember the doctor's name, but I'll never forget what she said: "Mrs. Clancy, I'm sorry, but it's cancer on *both* sides." The preliminary diagnosis, pending an MRI and further tests: Stage II.

My whole body jerked backward, like somebody had thrust a snake in my face. *Nuh-unh-unh, no way*, I thought. I don't remember a whole lot after that. "Blah-blah-blah," is what I heard the doctor say. The Nurse Navigator brought us a plastic bag filled with brochures about treatments and options. I took it, but I was still thinking, *We don't need that, we don't have cancer*. And then I cried. I bawled. John cried a little bit, too. I don't remember how long we sat there, but at some point I said, "Your tissues suck, you guys! They are so rough."

I'd only told my work friend and my sister about the biopsy. My sister must have called about ten times to check in, but I couldn't answer the phone. I just couldn't talk. The next time it rang, I gave the phone to John. He said, "Hello," and then broke up. He finally regained control, and when he told my sister the diagnosis, I could hear her wail like a wounded animal. John held the phone away from his ear. The whole thing was a horror, and not the best first reaction you want after telling someone you have cancer.

We didn't know how to tell our kids. We wanted to be casual about the news so the boys wouldn't be too scared. "It isn't too bad," I said. "They'll probably do chemo. It's gonna be okay."

That was our plan, and although plans might change, I believe I always need a plan. Ours was to act as normally as possible. We might have been a little too lighthearted, though, because afterward, Kevin, our high school sophomore, said, "So can I go to a party tonight?" I laughed and said, "No, I think you should stay home tonight." It hadn't hit him yet, but it would, and I didn't want him to be out.

Having breast cancer didn't seem like a death sentence to me. My family had no history of the disease, and genetic testing revealed no predisposition. I had breast-fed my children, I had started my period late—all generally indicators that you will not get breast cancer. When we went out to eat, I'd order turkey when everybody else ordered steak. Drinking too much alcohol can be a factor, but does that count if it was mainly during college? The whole thing just seemed so weird and wrong.

When you get sick, everyone who cares about you wants to know all the details. I couldn't handle repeating the same story over and over when I couldn't even tell it to myself. I told everything to my friend Margie and asked her to let everybody else know. The next night she invited John and me to their house to play cards. Her husband, Bill, trumped me. Instinctively, I piped up and said, "Hey, no fair: I have cancer!" It just came out of my mouth. Bill said, "Oh God, here she goes!" We all cracked up. For the first time John and I believed that we could make fun of my condition and beat it. We could have power over the cancer as long as we didn't let it terrify us.

The next day I had to photograph two anniversary Masses, a twenty-fifth and a fiftieth, for the Catholic newspaper. I was in a slight daze—that in-between, out of phase time, before the shit hits the fan. I snapped pictures, thinking that no one had any clue that I had cancer. The ceremony's homily was about being with your spouse for twenty-five and fifty years, and part of me wondered, *Oh crap, am I going to get to be with John for fifty years?*

That afternoon I wrote an e-mail with the subject line "I need my girlfriends" and sent it to everybody on my e-mail list.

You might have already heard that on Friday I learned I have breast cancer. Tomorrow I'm going to find out what stage it is and how the doctors plan to treat it. I need my girlfriends. John and the boys are going to be at Boy Scouts from 5 to 7 tonight. Anybody who wants to come by, bring some wine or whatever.

About forty-five girls and a couple of guys came over. I was euphoric, like "I have my girlfriends and my husband and my boys, and we are gonna beat this!" One friend attributed my mood to too much wine, but I'd had only one glass. Some friends said I didn't complain *enough*, but when I did, they'd say, "Oh, sweets, we're so sorry for you." I didn't like that.

I put on a positive face for the world, but in private I cried almost every day—on purpose. I forced myself to tears in the shower every morning, before putting on my makeup, before I went out to greet the day. It was a premeditated release, not a weakness. I let the fear and the hurt out. It was like girls and "chick flicks." Sometimes we just need to cry a little, let it out, and then we feel better.

None of this was easy, but thank goodness I didn't have to depend on only myself for strength. The rest came from God, and from my husband and my kids. I'm always thinking, *God, don't let me die, I can't leave them.*

The MRI revealed how bad the cancer really was. It had already spread to the lymph nodes in both breasts. The tumor in my left breast was only two millimeters. But the tumor in my right breast, which had been hidden in the fibrocystic tissue, was 5.2 centimeters. Huge. The doctors reset my condition as Stage III and planned for a double mastectomy. John almost lost it. He knew how serious this was. He put his head down and moaned. Now I had to be strong for John, and inside I felt oddly empowered. Being at Stage III meant that I'd need more aggressive chemo, more aggressive radiation. I felt like, "Cool! Let's kick the cancer's butt!"

That attitude stuck. When I told one lady at school that I had cancer, she asked if she could tell other people. I said, "You know me: If I'm going through it, eventually we're all going through it."

My friend Margie had been diagnosed with breast cancer the year before. Her phone rang all the time. Her kids would roll their eyeballs every time she'd go into the bedroom again, shut the door, and tell the story. The night we'd played cards at her house, I asked if she could find a way for me to let everyone know what's going on, using the computer. "I saw what you went through. I can't keep saying all this over and over. It brings me down. I'm too busy. I've got my life to save."

Margie helped me sign up at CaringBridge. I treated my journal as a conversation between me and my friends, and it kept me going. We could as easily exchange posts about coffee creamers and bra shopping as about my illness. Some of my friends would complain about airport security or ramble on about their families. Others would talk about sports and recipes. And best of all, these exchanges kept my mind off chemo.

Once, I posted a list of "Reasons That I Have to Be Happy Tonight." Among them:

- I figured out a way to take a bath today and not get my port wet!!! (I had been going on three weeks of sponge bathing and washing my hair in the sink!)
- My CaringBridge buddy, Rebecca, who's going through her own chemo, prayed for ME today in her journal. Her faith and insight are unbelievable.
- (My son) Kevin finished his senior thesis tonight! I'm thankful that God has given our children the gift of intelligence. Hopefully they're going to use that gift to get through exams this week!
- Wendy (our dog) started eating again yesterday! She had not eaten since Tuesday, and was worrying us so much! Her cough is gone, but she's still very lethargic, so she's going to see the vet again tomorrow.
- AND...the number one reason that I'm feeling happy tonight...The infection is looking better!!! I'll see Dr. Peterson Tuesday morning, and he will decide if he needs to order another week of IV or not. I'll keep you updated!

On the other hand, if I was upset in the middle of the night, I could be open with my feelings and depend on support. One time I had to have a blood transfusion and I didn't know what that meant. I was terrified. So I wrote about it and it wasn't long before five people wrote back saying, "Oh Traci, you'll feel better afterward, don't worry." Within about two hours I was okay about the transfusion, whereas otherwise I might have been up all night scared to death, and crying. That's how CaringBridge helped me: by putting me in easy contact with my friends.

Several people have since told me that they found out they had breast cancer after they read my journal, and are more comfortable going through the treatment themselves because they'd been through it with me.

But a couple of friends said, "You write too much. We just want to know if everything is okay." So one day I wrote, "For KK and L: Everything's fine. You can quit reading now. Everyone else, keep reading."

One friend didn't want to go online. She said, "I don't read your journal because I'd rather hear it from you. How can I help you?" Finally I said, "The way you can help me is by reading my journal. It's very hard for me to say these things over and over." Then she started reading and said, "Oh, now I see."

Sometimes readers would judge me. If someone didn't want to read what I'd written, fine. No big deal. I wrote—and still write—for people who want to know what's going on, not for attention. I'd tell my boys, "When that visitor number goes up, that's another prayer."

I've had people tell me, "Traci, I read your journal every day, but I don't write anything because I'm too shy." That was completely fine.

A girl from Washington, DC, e-mailed me to say she'd found my CaringBridge journal and had been reading it all day. She explained that she never went out of the house, because she didn't want to get germs, but she'd gotten so depressed that her husband was worried. After reading my journal she wanted to try to change. That's so cool to me.

Using the dialogue between my journal and the guest book I think I've been able to make cancer a gift for other people, and I know that it has made me appreciate life much more. John and I have had some money problems. In the middle of chemo we found out one of our sons had ADD. We made it through, and getting through cancer meant we could get through anything. Of course we all still argue and get annoyed with one another, but we know deep down we've been through hell—and come back.

My body stood up to all the treatments so well that my doctor called me a poster girl for chemo. It wasn't what I'd aimed for, but I was happy to get the feedback. My hair fell out and my toenails came off, and a lot of the time I felt like crap, but from talking to other cancer survivors I realized that my symptoms and side effects weren't as bad as they could have been. I got numbness in my fingers for a while, but some people's whole hands get numb and stay that way. I never even got constipated! I didn't want to listen to the doctor tell me about possible side effects because I thought knowing about them would make them appear, and later I'd say, "Is that something you told me might happen? I do have it now."

One part of having breast cancer wasn't that great, of course: the mastectomies. A friend who had Stage I breast cancer had only a teeny tiny scar on the side of her boob. I overheard her telling someone, "Go for the mastectomy; you'll have pretty new boobs." I interrupted her and said, "Mine aren't very pretty." But I only needed Barbie bumps. I don't care, and my husband forgets. I'll be naked and he'll look at me and say, "Oh, cool." I'll say, "Really?" and he'll say, "I don't care." We're still intimate, and I think he's forgotten what my other breasts looked like. I've pretty much forgotten myself, when I have clothes on.

Because of the affected lymph nodes I have some lymphedema

in the right side of my torso, right around where my bra sits. It comes from having had forty-five or sixty staples across my back where they flipped part of my back muscle up to form my right breast, and now there's a fluid buildup that causes swelling. I had to wear a compression garment for a while, and it still feels like there's something stuck there. I got some tattoo sleeves to be fashionable: They're called lympheDIVAs.

It's been four years, and I don't have any cancer now. When I reach five years, I can quit taking the medicine. That's kind of scary because if estrogen-positive cancer comes back, it's most likely to happen *after* the five-year mark. It returned and metastasized in a friend after a nine-year remission. She survived another six years and passed away very recently. I know I might not totally beat cancer, but maybe because of the national drive for cancer awareness, my boys won't have to go through with their wives what their father went through with me. So many girls are now aware of breast cancer. Girls today start self-checks at twenty, and mammograms at forty. I explained that to my youngest son, Patrick, but he said, "Mom, duh! When we're forty, there's not going to be breast cancer." Good job, Patrick!

My friend and neighbor, a chemo nurse, recently confided in me: "Traci, I don't tell everybody this because I find that many people don't want to hear my thoughts on God, but you're my neighbor and my friend. I have dreams sometimes about water. If someone is in a dream with water, I feel like it's a good and healing thing; it's God and it's powerful. I had a dream about you last night, and you were surrounded by water. I've never had a dream where anybody had *so much* water around them. You are going to do good. You're going to be okay and you're going to help people."

I can only hope so. The cancer was sometimes so inconvenient. It so messed with my life. But I know that I've helped other people because of my experience, and if I can continue to do that, I'll feel great. To remind myself, I've tacked a fortune-cookie fortune on my refrigerator: "Turn your scars into stars."

You know me: I'm making a plan.

Remembering the Golden Rule

When a coworker is exhausted from juggling the demands of work, children, and caring for an ailing parent, we all know a few frozen home-cooked meals would ease the burden, yet we often don't act. When a neighbor is home after surgery, we sometimes tell ourselves, "She probably needs her rest right now."

And yet, for any of us who have stood on the other side of difficult times—medical, emotional, or financial—we know that there is nothing more useful nor more healing than the hand that reaches out.

When someone cares enough to notice we could use a hand, are we concerned that protocol is followed, or are we thankful for their grip? When we find ourselves in need, are we concerned that information comes only from pedigreed experts, or are we simply grateful when wisdom comes our way? The "I've been there too…" from a colleague whose path rarely crosses ours, or the neighbor mowing our lawn, or the gift of a cleaning service just before the swarm of holiday visitors—those are the things that get us through.

The person who needs you right now might be your neighbor, your student, your client, or your patient. It might even be a competitor or a stranger. We all wear many hats and move in many circles. Those roles and lines need not be walls. The intersection of generosity and gratefulness trumps awkwardness every time.

PAULA COULTER

I Want My Old Life Back

Interstate highway bridges are not supposed to fall.

On August 1, 2007, my husband, Brad, our daughters Brianna and Brandi, and I were crossing the I-35 West bridge in our Honda Odyssey, on the way to meet my sisters and their families for burgers and beer. Brianna and her cousin Tyler were leaving for college the next week, and this was our little celebration. I sat in the back with Brandi; Brianna took the front passenger seat; Brad drove. We were running late, and Brad was trying to make up time. I asked Brianna to please put on her seat belt—she did—while I called my sister to tell her we'd be late. Then I closed my eyes to catch a quick nap while we fought through Minneapolis rush-hour traffic.

We had almost made it across when the roadway began to ripple and shake. Brad floored the gas pedal, but the bridge just crumbled beneath us, and scant yards from safety, our van went airborne, flipped on its back, fell sixty-five feet, and landed upside down on the riverbank below. All the windows blew out and the air bags inflated. Despite their injuries, Brandi and Brianna were able to crawl out their respective windows. Brad made it out his window, desperately motivated by his claustrophobia. But when he looked back at the hopelessly crushed van, I was still hanging from my seat belt, barely conscious.

Thirteen people died that afternoon, and another 145 were injured. Along the span, cars fell into the water and sank. Big trucks burst into flames. A school bus came to rest along a cantilevered edge and got stuck there. A construction person fell face-first into the mud. The legs of a young woman driving the car in front of us were pinned and crushed by concrete. Others were caught and obliterated under massive slabs of roadway. From the pictures I saw later, it looked like Godzilla had tossed the bridge around like a toy.

When I opened my eyes, I was lying in a hospital bed. My sister Lisa sat by my side. "How long do you think you've been here?" she asked.

"I don't know," I said. "Two or three days?"

"No," she said. "It's been five weeks."

I suppose I'm one of the lucky ones; I'm not dead. But not a day goes by that I don't wonder what my life would have been like had the accident never happened. I'd give anything, any money, to go back to how my life was before.

I had a good life. We're a normal, close-knit, Christian family. I'm an accountant and had just gotten a promotion. My new job would be to help my company implement new software in thirty-seven states. I worked out five days a week and ran four or five miles each day. Our daughter Brianna was a high school senior on her way to Winona State College on a soccer scholarship. Brandi was a high school junior and also played soccer. Brad worked at Jostens.

One of the first ambulances to arrive took me to the Hennepin County Medical Center (HCMC), where they rushed me into surgery. I had a brain injury—the doctors later said I had probably slammed my head into the hook above the back door that holds clothes hangers—and my L1 vertebra was also crushed. The surgeon removed a bone flap from my skull so my swollen brain could expand without increasing my intercranial pressure. My heart failed on the operating table, and the CPR that revived me somehow broke a rib, which then punctured a lung.

Brianna and Brandi were also triaged to HCMC, Brianna in the back of a pickup truck and Brandi in an ambulance with four other people. Brad left in a fire truck, then was transferred to an ambulance headed for North Memorial Hospital. My injuries were critical, but Brandi told me that before the ambulance took me away, she couldn't stop crying, and though I don't remember this, I was conscious enough to tell her, "Don't worry. We're going to be okay. I love you."

Brad had five fractured vertebrae, and the girls each had two. All left the hospital within a week with neck and back braces they wore for months. I remained behind.

After I woke up, I couldn't speak, because I'd had a tracheostomy, but the doctors inserted a small valve that let me say a few words—and a few days later they closed up the wound so I could speak on my own. I asked what had happened, but no one really wanted to go into detail. They called it "a car accident." Eventually they told me about the bridge. It took months before

I knew the extent of the chaos and damage. When I finally saw pictures of our van, on its roof, the back end crushed, the front end mashed, I thought we should have all perished.

———

My husband, Brad, had known about CaringBridge, and my brother-in-law Craig decided to start the page because no one in our immediate family could. It was a great way to communicate about my condition and progress. Once I was awake, I read the journal. It was weird to read about what had happened to me and about the time I spent in a medically induced coma.

> *"Paula is still in critical condition, and the doctors continue to stress the first seventy-two critical hours. We're just looking to weather that milestone and go from there."*
>
> *"Paula did have the ventilator removed around 9:30 this morning. She is breathing successfully on her own, but it is probably not permanent, as there is an impending surgery for her back. I understand that this may take place Tuesday morning. But, that's been changed a few times already, so things remain dynamic."*

My husband, Brad, had e-mailed Craig to ask him to post this letter to the site:

> *WOW, where do you begin? I guess you start by saying, "We are lucky to be alive!!" As I sit here looking at pictures and trying to digest the last week, I can only sit in awe. It is amazing how four seconds can change the course of your life. To my wife, who I love dearly, I only wish that I could take your place, so that*

you wouldn't have to endure any more suffering. To my kids, who I adore, I am very proud of you for staying calm and strong for your mother and me. To my family and friends, "WE ARE BLESSED." We would not be able to do it without you. The outpouring of love and support has me in tears right now. There are too many people to name that have stepped up and taken charge to make sure all the little things are taken care of for us. People we don't even know have dropped off groceries or even a Starbucks card for a simple coffee (Minnesota nice, I guess). It truly makes me cry (and I am not usually a breakdown kind of guy, ask Paula). Each of our companies (Jostens and The Mentor Network) have been so supportive. It's not every day you get a call from your CEO asking and caring how you are doing and not to worry about anything. (Thanks, Mike!) There are many people to thank, but also a long ways to go. My priority is to get Paula (Effie is her nickname) home and well again. I do not know how to thank you all for the outpouring of love and support, but I will find a way to repay it in time. I read all of the entries in the guest book, and we are so lucky to have such a network for friends, many I have not heard from in years and well-wishers I don't even know.

I was also inspired by what my visitors had written. I felt their love and support in the guest book. My self-confidence and motivation improved, and I knew I wouldn't see negative input. In fact, my mother wouldn't let anyone take pictures of me during my recuperation because she thought that it would really upset me. Even when my brother-in-law Craig wanted to shoot a few frames for the record, she put her foot down. "She's not going to want to see herself like this. I think it's a mistake."

My big goal from the very beginning was to get back to normal. I had to be the person I was before the accident. I assumed it would take a year. While Brad dealt with the medical insurance, the investigative committees, the lawyers, the car, our daughters, their injuries, me, and the real world, I kept asking when I'd be at 100 percent again. What could he say?

Rehab has to be the slowest, most difficult process there is. Advances are tiny and, fortunately, cumulative. Setbacks are depressing. Patience is the mantra. I went through all the stages: learning to transfer to and from bed, using a wheelchair, tentative first steps, using a continuous passive motion machine and other exercise machines, time in the pool. As tough as the physical aspects of rehab were, the cognitive tests also drove me crazy. I don't believe I could have answered those questions *before* I fell off the bridge. "We're going to say eight words and we want you to say the eight words, then we're going to do a couple more things, then we're going to come back and I want you to tell me what the eight words are. Then we're going to add a few words, do something else, then come back."

Just before Christmas, I returned home, but physical therapy continued. I'd make headway, and we wanted to maintain those results over time, but sometimes the results wore off in an hour. I still had major problems. Bone grew in unexpected places, calcifying in my muscles. I had three surgeries to remove painful spurs. I had bladder issues. My right leg and hip wouldn't stop hurting. My range of motion remained limited. The doctors implanted a pump to manage nerve pain. I walked with difficulty and tired very easily. And yet I clung to my dream of being able to run again, and had to keep reminding myself that I had good reason to be positive: the doctors had once believed I might be permanently brain-damaged and disabled, or at best have emotional mood swings and cry for no reason at all.

Sometimes I just wanted to lie in bed because that's where my body hurt the least. Instead, I styled my hair. I put on makeup and nail polish. I talked to reporters about the accident. I got a tattoo like Brianna and Brandi had. The tattoo is of a Chinese word meaning "trust" or "believe," and the date of the bridge collapse: August 1, 2007. I was on some good drugs when they did that. When they wore off, I said, "Oh my God, this hurts!" I went with my daughters to Mexico for Spring Break 2008. I watched Brianna graduate.

I had great difficulty accepting how my injuries had and would affect my life. I wanted to wish myself better. When a year had passed—by then the state had built a new bridge and there was a ceremony and survivor interviews—I realized that a year wouldn't be enough to make me normal again. In the spirit of being fair and patient I added another year to my timetable. I wanted to run, but first I had to walk. My new goal was to look like anyone else, not injured, when I went out for a stroll.

A year after the accident I felt compelled to reread my CaringBridge site once more. I guess I needed a shot of inspiration. Starting at the beginning was very therapeutic. I smiled and cried and felt loved all over again, especially when I read this entry by Brad:

"I am SO proud of you and have never doubted your drive and desire to get better. You will be home with us very soon. I try to

be there for you as much as possible to give you encouragement and to make sure you keep up the positive attitude. YOU ARE MY ROCK!! I get strength from watching you work hard every day and always having the "WHAT DO YOU WANT ME TO DO NEXT?" attitude with your therapists. Keep up the good work and all will be back to normal soon."

Eighteen months after the accident I wanted to go back to work. Our lawyers and one of my recovery physicians wanted me to meet with a neuropsych physician first, to determine whether there were any lingering issues. I got a call from the neuropsych to schedule an appointment. I remembered the maddening mental twisters of rehab. "I am not happy to come and see you," I said.

His office was in the same building as my work. His assistant did the first two hours of testing, and then I had lunch with my work colleagues on the fifth floor. I came back down to finish the rest of the tests and, to my surprise, I liked the doctor, probably for two reasons: He seemed like a nice person, and this time I'd been able to answer his questions, because I was further into my recovery. This time I didn't feel like such an idiot.

It's been five years since the bridge collapse, and mentally I'm fine, but physically I'm *still* not at 100 percent. Eighty-five, maybe. But this is good. I've discovered that I have the right combination of personality and attitude for the long haul. And I'm running again. Not normal running, but as best as I can. Three years after the accident I ran a 5K race—very carefully. My time was fifty-four minutes. Last summer I did it in thirty-eight minutes.

Unfortunately, last fall I fell on my butt, in my bedroom of all places, and had a 70 percent tear in the meniscus of my knee. This setback couldn't have come at a more inopportune time, and I felt worse about it than just about anything I've had to deal with so far. Good news: my orthopedist would be able to repair it. Bad news: I have Grade 3 arthritis. I had surgery to fix it, and three months later I was back in his examination room because it still hurt like hell. A cortisone shot helped. My knee is now 95 percent back, and I pray it's not bad luck to say so.

My biggest fear going forward is that I'll be hit worse and earlier with all the deterioration that happens to us naturally as we age. I'm afraid it's going to take very little for things to go wrong. Injuries require surgery, and surgery creates its own side effects and setbacks that sometimes become permanent. I have hip problems as well as back problems, and lingering effects from my brain injury. I bought a bicycle recently and was surprised that I had to relearn how to ride it because I have balance problems. It's *not* just as easy as getting on the bike again.

Today the girls go to St. Catherine University in Saint Paul, study health care, and play on the soccer team, and Brad and I are empty-nesters. We've always been a close family, particularly my girls and me, just because we're females, and we've always done things together. But now everyone is even closer and we share an important outlook on life: we're not indispensable. Brad has been a huge, huge, huge, huge help to me, and I know that's because our love has always been strong and that he did what came naturally.

I've read and heard many stories in which people who go through life-changing situations—from illness to accident and more—say that the problem became a gift. I understand what they mean, and have seen the positive results in others, but I have never felt that way. Not yet, anyway. Nor do I feel bad for believing that.

I did an interview with the Minneapolis *Star Tribune* for the five-year anniversary of the bridge collapse, and when Brad mentioned that I'd almost died, the reporter said, "And you're *smiling?*"

Yes, I'm smiling. I'm here. I'm alive. But I would still give the world to have my old life back.

"People expect anyone who has cancer to be miserable. Of course, I had lots of low days. At first I immediately imagined myself six feet under. But I tried not to talk about how awful I felt. I probably shed more tears after my diagnosis than I had in my entire life, but I didn't share my private despair or questions about whether or not I'd survive. I'm generally a high-energy, positive person. I try to look at not only the bright but also the funny side of life. I read early on that cancer patients who have a cheerful attitude tend to do better. I also like people and want to connect with them. You don't connect when you're miserable.

"I know I'm lucky. My story is not like some of the nightmares I've heard. Some women don't make it. Still, I'd say: Appreciate every day. Stay positive. Try to look for the silver lining in the clouds. I believe that my positive attitude is a big reason why my tumor is gone."

—*Wendy Buchanan, breast cancer survivor*

MINDY FAST

I'm Still Here

It's hard for me to remember my life before cancer.

My daughter was twelve and my son was nine when I was diagnosed. I was active in the PTA and very involved with the kids. I had a master's degree in math and worked part-time at the same job I have now, as a bookkeeper in our local synagogue. When I was forty, I saw my gynecologist and he recommended a physical. I'd been thinking about that myself, but hadn't gotten around to scheduling it. I was busy. He ordered blood work to get me started.

When the results came back, everything—I do mean everything—was out of the normal range. The doctor thought it must be a mistake and ordered a second series of blood tests, but somehow I knew it was going to be bad. And again, everything was abnormal.

My internist referred me to another doctor, who referred me to Dr. David Siegel at Morristown Memorial Hospital, just twenty minutes from my house in New Jersey. Meeting him turned out to be such a blessing.

Dr. Siegel specialized in treating multiple myeloma, a cancer of the plasma cells in the bone marrow, which is what he thought I had. In 2001, multiple myeloma had a three- to five-year life expectancy. Dr. Siegel described it, saying that your stem cells develop into red cells, white cells, and platelets, and produce bone marrow. If something goes wrong at one step of the way in that production, it's leukemia. If at another step, it's lymphoma. At another step, it's myeloma. Going a little further, he explained that the blood has immunoglobulins, which we laypeople usually call antibodies. There are immunoglobulins A, M, and G, referred to as IG-A, IG-M, and IG-G. With myeloma, one of them starts cloning itself out of control.

IG-A levels should normally be in the very low hundreds. Mine was in the thousands. Your blood should contain less than 5 percent plasma cells. Mine was about 70 percent plasma cells, leaving no room for all the other stuff that had to be there. My cholesterol was 111—a great number for a healthy person to have. But for me it was artificially low because of the myeloma. To say I was devastated by all my numbers and what they implied is an understatement.

My husband and I wanted a second opinion, and Dr. Siegel recommended a doctor he had no connection with, at the Dana-Farber Cancer Institute in Boston. My parents came up to watch the kids, whom we'd already told about my condition, but not in a way that sounded so serious that they'd think I might die. The doctor at Dana-Farber examined me and confirmed the original diagnosis, then added that Dr. Siegel was "one of the best doctors in the country." We could trust him.

The next time I met with Dr. Siegel, I told him I was planning a bat mitzvah for my daughter, and I said, "My son is only nine. I need to see him graduate high school."

"That's the plan," he said, and showed me a treatment plan

that would let me have the bat mitzvah. Thereafter, each visit to Dr. Siegel would start with him asking, "How are the bat mitzvah plans going? How are the kids?"

After the celebration the heavy-duty chemotherapy would begin, to prepare me to have my stem cells harvested and returned. He also put me on high doses of steroids and thalidomide, the drug from the 1960s that caused birth defects. When you're premenopausal and on thalidomide, you have to take a pregnancy test every month. Still, I got a call from the manufacturer, who said I needed to be on *two* kinds of birth control. I said, "I have cancer. Do you think I'm going to get pregnant?! That's my birth control. I've got cancer and I feel horrible."

Thalidomide is a really hard drug to tolerate. You get constipated like you can't imagine. Your whole digestive tract just stops, you have to take laxatives twice a day, and if that doesn't work for a couple of days you have to... Let's just say it was horrible. I alternated four days on high doses of steroids and four days off. Steroids boost the effects of the chemo. They also make you feel like you've chugged twenty cups of coffee at once. I babbled out of control, aware of what was happening but unable to stop. The four days off made me crash. My legs become achy and heavy, and I had absolutely no energy. I was like a zombie. A very slow zombie. Just as that would start to taper off, I'd have to start taking the steroids again.

The routine clouded my mind, and it was all I could do to focus on my three part-time jobs: bookkeeping, the bat mitzvah, and the cancer. When I shopped with my daughter for a bat mitzvah dress, I leaned against the wall, feeling miserable, but forced myself to smile. Two days after the ceremony I started the chemotherapy that would make me lose my hair in the name of trying to obliterate the cancer. I got a catheter attached to a bag that had to be refilled with chemicals at the hospital every day for five days. After that, my stem cells would be harvested from my blood, I'd get even higher doses of chemo, and wait to get my stem cells back. I wanted my hair back, too, but I had to be patient.

At the stem cell harvesting, my nurses were switching out my catheter when the doctor looked up from his paperwork and said, "We can't harvest her stem cells yet. Her platelets are at eight"—meaning 8,000. Anything below 50,000 puts you at extreme risk of bleeding to death from even a minor bump. I needed a platelet transfusion to get the number up. Also, my white cell count had to be 3.0, and it was 0.3. They sent me home.

The next day my white count was 0.6. They sent me home again.

The next day was July 4 and I didn't have to go to the hospital. But I had zero to celebrate.

Two days later my white count was 2.9. Almost! They said, "On Monday you'll be good to go." I hoped so. I also took a double dose of Neupogen, a drug that boosts white cell and stem cell production. The side effect is intense bone pain. But on Monday, my white count was 52. Incredibly high. Good to go.

A successful harvest is 25 million stem cells. This typically takes a week. But when I returned for my second day, the nurse said, "We tried to reach you, but you'd already left the house. We got the twenty-five million. You're done." My nurses hugged me and cheered. Now I just had to go home and wait until my stem cells could return home, too.

I had a couple of weeks to recover, during which I discovered that some hospitals now offer "complementary medicine." They do massage and other healing therapies. I called the

Complementary-Medicine Program and said, "I don't know what I need, but I need something." The technician said, "Oh, you want Jin Shin Jyutsu." O-kay? Turns out that you lie fully clothed on your back and they lightly touch you in different places. The philosophy is that there are twenty-six safety energy locks in our body, and whenever you have any kind of ailment—a cold, a toothache, cancer—it's because one or more of these safety energy locks are blocked. They touch you in different combinations—one hand on your knee, the other hand on your shoulder—to open the locks. I did it once. Did it help? I don't know. But it was very nice to lie there and be touched gently.

I also went to multiple myeloma and stem cell support groups at the hospital. At the myeloma support group I met a woman who was probably in her seventies. She'd had a transplant and called it, "the Dr. Siegel Adventure." I thought if she could get through it okay, I should be able to as well.

A transplant is not my definition of fun. I spent two weeks in semi-isolation. My visitors were limited and they had to wear masks; however, nausea and vomiting were allowed to visit often. I couldn't shower or drink tap water. I used warm baby wipes to wash myself. My husband came to see me every day and took care of the laundry and grocery shopping at home—a big challenge for him. Friends brought meals, but he even did some cooking. Amazing.

The transplant returned my blood-work number to near normal, and although a month or two later the numbers began to climb again slightly, I didn't get treatment. I went back to work at the synagogue, and for a year I was monitored. I didn't tell my parents anything—though they knew I had cancer, of course—because we wanted to spare them extra stress and didn't want my condition blown out of proportion by their worry. I went back to my gynecologist a year after he had sent me for the blood work, and I said, "I don't know if I should thank you for doing the blood work that found the cancer, or hate you because this has been hard, and once upon a time I had a really nice life."

One day Dr. Siegel told me he was leaving Morristown Memorial but was moving to nearby Hackensack Hospital. He wanted to get me into a clinical trial for a new drug, but because of the bureaucracy it couldn't start for another year. Meanwhile I was off treatment, not doing particularly well, but not feeling horribly sick either. I could function, and I carried on with a brave face.

I finally got into the clinical trial, and at first it seemed like a miracle. After just one cycle of treatment I came as close to remission as I'd ever been. Then the drug just stopped working. I had to go back to the thalidomide and steroid regimen. Dr. Siegel adjusted my dosages, but as soon as he reduced them, the cancer became more active. I started taking Revlimid, the second generation of thalidomide. It was a thousand times more effective without the drowsiness or the horrible constipation. Once again I allowed myself to be hopeful. Every time I had a treatment, like with the first transplant, I thought, *Okay, this cancer is behind me now.* A month later: *Oh, I guess it's not.*

Nothing ever put me into remission. I wasn't in control or out of control. My cancer and I just plodded along.

Eventually Dr. Siegel suggested a second transplant, this time using donor stem cells. We had talked about it earlier, but I'd rejected the idea outright. Finding a donor can be a very long and discouraging process, and there can be dangerous side effects to putting someone else's stem cells in your body. Now it was time, but once again I needed to delay. "I'll do it if I can wait a couple years until my son starts college," I said.

"That would be too late," Dr. Siegel said.

When I announced I was having a second transplant, my friends said, "Oh! The cancer is back?" They didn't realize it had never gone away. But I didn't feel any shame about being ill. There are too many people with cancer to feel that way. I knew a woman my age who died because she stopped going to the doctor. She had myeloma, and her first transplant was successful. When her doctor moved, she didn't follow him and she didn't go to another doctor. Eventually the cancer came back. She e-mailed me about her problems, and I urged her to go see Dr. Siegel. But she waited until she was so sick that they couldn't save her. It's so important to listen to your doctor!

Dr. Siegel and I scheduled the transplant for the coming summer, when my son would be between his junior and senior years in high school. I thought it would be easier then. In retrospect I should have waited until he actually started his senior year, when he was busy with school and constantly around friends, who could drive him wherever he needed or wanted to go. We had a difficult summer, but he was pretty clear about what was happening to me and was very understanding.

My daughter went through a typical teenage period, when she wanted me out of her life—not knowing, of course, what that really meant, even if I had never been sick. Kids don't think it through. She thought I was a horrible mother. What else is new? She was thirteen and probably scared.

I'm not sure how graphic I was with the kids about the cancer this time. I didn't hide it, but I didn't make an issue of it. They knew, when I went in for the second transplant, that it was serious, but they didn't feel I might die and didn't pass along a negative attitude. Sometimes I overheard them saying, "Mom's always sick," but I still took them to ball games and classes, cooked their dinner, did the grocery shopping. Their lives were not really affected.

I needed a stem cell donor. My son volunteered, my daughter didn't. My sister, with whom I'm very close, wasn't a match. I was very concerned, but the doctor didn't foresee any problem finding a match for someone with my ethnic background. Jews tend to register as donors. They found nineteen people who matched on the initial six criteria. Of those, usually one of nine is a perfect match. I got lucky.

I still have no idea who she was. She chose to remain anonymous, which really upsets me. All I know is that my donor is a woman who had been pregnant only once. I asked my doctor why that mattered. He said, "Every time you're pregnant, your body produces antibodies." The more antibodies, the worse it would have been for me.

I wrote to the woman after the transplant and said, "Thank you, thank you, thank you!" I wrote to her again when I found out that I was in remission. "How do I thank you? Oh my God, you gave me *life*!"

I had to wait a year after the transplant to be allowed to give her all my identifying information: name, address, telephone, e-mail. I wrote again and passed the letter through the appropriate channels. I've never heard anything. I even followed up once, wanting to make sure that she had received my messages. They checked and told me, "Yes, she did. Some people choose to remain anonymous."

It's frustrating. I'd love to know who she is.

But I did find out about someone else.

I used CaringBridge strictly for the transplant and wrote only thirty posts. Friends of ours whose son had brain cancer told us about it. I tried to set up my site using my name, but a message popped up: "That name is taken. Please choose another." I added my middle name: Mindy Sue Fast. I posted every day that I was in the hospital and then a few times after, but how much could I say about how I was walking a little bit, hurt one day, felt better the other, and otherwise mostly sat around. However, the support and the outpourings of love in the guest book were amazing. They gave me a lot of strength.

One day a woman signed my guest book, "the other Mindy Fast." I'd had a feeling, because a few weeks before the post appeared, a nurse had called me about the donor search and said, "We're looking for a match on the registry for you. I thought you said your sister was tested."

I said, "She was. She's not a match."

"I got a report that your brother was tested, too."

"I don't have a brother."

"Well, it says here that your brother was tested."

"But I'm telling you, I don't have a brother."

The nurse insisted. "He was tested in Virginia." Then she paused and said, "Oh. This Mindy Fast has a different date of birth. It's not you."

I asked my husband if he had a cousin named Mindy who lived in Virginia. He said yes, but that she was married and wouldn't be a Fast anymore. The nurse had unwittingly violated HIPAA, so, although we were intrigued—this Mindy apparently had the same condition I did, hence the testing—I said, "Let's just drop it. We don't want to start asking family. Maybe this Mindy doesn't want people to know."

But then she wrote on my guest book.

Within a few days, "the other Mindy Fast" called me. She had talked with one of her cousins in New Jersey, who somehow knew about me. We had so many things in common. She is a little bit older than I am, but we've been married the same number of years. Her kids are each one year older than my two. And, most unbelievably, we had the same disease. We e-mailed and called each other often. We could discuss with each other the side effects that you don't talk about with other people. Several months later my husband and I drove to Virginia to meet her, her husband, and her daughter. It was even great for the husbands, who were the caregivers, to talk to each other. You know the word *beshert*? It means something is destined to be. It was *beshert* that we found each other.

I never went to Hebrew school, my family didn't go to temple, but I've always identified strongly as Jewish. In college, I went to services more often and became much more involved. When my kids were old enough for Hebrew school, I thought that I couldn't send them if I didn't know anything, so I started learning the language. During the treatment for my first transplant, I promised myself that if I survived, I would have my own bat mitzvah.

I made it through that transplant, but didn't know how I could have a bat mitzvah at my age, until my synagogue offered an adult b'nai mitzvah class. Unfortunately, it was scheduled to last well after the summer when my second transplant was scheduled. Who knew what kind of shape I'd be in by then? I had to speed things up.

I found a tape from my daughter's bat mitzvah, I learned how to read Torah, and at the beginning of the summer I had a full-fledged bat mitzvah just like all the thirteen-year-olds. The Torah reading was particularly appropriate. The Jews leave Egypt, they wander the desert, they reach the outskirts of Canaan. Moses sends out twelve scouts. Ten of them come back and say, "Forget it! The Canaanites are big. There's no way we can beat them. Let's go back to Egypt and be slaves again." Two of the scouts say, "We can do this. God is saying we can do this."

I felt like God was saying I would make it through the summer and the second transplant. It was a very emotional day.

I'm still a regular Torah and Haftorah reader. My faith in Judaism has gotten stronger. Cancer made me want to go to temple more, to feel closer to God. God has seen me through all this. I draw my strength and inspiration from Him. I pray more. I talk to God more. I definitely am a believer.

I was diagnosed when I was forty years old. I'll be fifty-two in a month. I've been in remission now for four years. I enjoy every day I have, because I'm sure at some point I will need treatment again. Myeloma is not an all-or-nothing disease. Dr. Siegel said most likely it will be back, but there will be more and better drugs available. Already a new drug has been approved. Meanwhile, although I have occasional continuing issues, I celebrate the good days for as long as they last.

Sometimes I feel like everyone should have a debilitating illness for a short while, because it really makes you appreciate your health. I wasn't allowed to vacation or do anything wild and crazy for a while, because my immune system was suppressed. I'm so appreciative of feeling healthy and having energy now. I exercise much more than I ever did. I lift heavier weights and I try to work up a sweat every day. I feel like I'm in the best shape I've ever been in.

I saw my son graduate from high school. I saw him graduate from college, too. Now I'd like to see him get married. I'd like to see the grandchildren. I keep setting the bar further into the future.

I'm still here.

> "Faith is not the belief that God will do what you want. It is the belief that God will do what is right."
> —*Max Lucado*, He Still Moves Stones

CORY REMSBURG

Never Give Up

My name is Craig Remsburg. I'm here with my son, Sergeant First Class Cory Remsburg—Army Ranger, First Battalion, Seventy-fifth Ranger Regiment. When he was deployed to Afghanistan in support of Operation Enduring Freedom, I prayed for his safety, as any parent would. But I didn't worry much. This was his tenth deployment, which included earlier missions in support of Operation Iraqi Freedom. However, this time, while leading his unit on patrol, one of Cory's men stepped on an improvised explosive device (IED). As the blast and smoke cleared, protocol demanded an immediate welfare check. Everyone had taken shrapnel, one Ranger had lost a foot, and two soldiers were missing: Cory and the unfortunate man who'd stepped on the IED. As daylight broke, one of the search team noticed unusual objects in a nearby canal. It was Cory, facedown, and the remains of the other Ranger.

When Cory was seventeen and a half, he brought me a sheaf of papers to sign. He needed my consent to officially commit to joining the army when he turned eighteen, through the delayed-entry program. When I asked him why, he was straightforward: "I want to serve."

Cory was a popular kid, who played in the high school orchestra, jazz band, and marching band; he belonged to the German club and the varsity volleyball team. I had reservations about his decision—not about serving—but I believed he hadn't explored other options on the table, like college. When I told Cory I wasn't ready to sign, he got a little angry, but as in any good father-son relationship, you move on.

Six months later, at five thirty in the morning, the front door-bell rang. I couldn't imagine who'd drop by that early, and hoped it wasn't bad news. I opened the door to find an army recruiter in uniform. Before I could say a word, I heard Cory coming down the steps behind me, already dressed. "I don't need you to sign anymore, Dad," he said. "I'm eighteen now."

I didn't expect that from Cory, but I was more proud than angry. I did the only thing I could do: support him. "You're right," I said. "This is now your decision." I hugged Cory and wished him well, and said he should call if something came up. I told the recruiter, "Take care of him," and watched them leave.

In the army you go in at the bottom, the infantry, and that's where you'll end up if the path you want to take forward doesn't work out. Cory wanted to be an Army Ranger. All the Ranger wannabes go through the steps together: if you pass basic training, Airborne school is next. If you make it, you enter the Ranger Indoctrination Program: RIP. Black humor. If you manage to graduate, and only 2 percent of those who try do, you get the Ranger scroll, but not the Ranger tab, which is yellow and black and says Ranger. Finally, you go to one of three Ranger units, the First, Second, and Third Battalions. Cory was assigned to the First Battalion, in Savannah, Georgia, at Hunter Army Airfield.

Cory and his group were in basic training when 9/11 happened. His first deployment was Iraq. He's since had ten deployments, and is a three-time volunteer: to be in the military, to be Airborne, and to be a Ranger. He's reenlisted twice. The first lasted four years. The second one was six. It's a career. It's a brotherhood.

CORY: Camaraderie.

After the explosion, other Rangers attended to the injured and secured the scene with no idea whether the enemy was lurking, or ready to attack. Cory and the Ranger who had stepped on the IED were pulled out of the canal and into the bomb crater, which would protect them while they worked to save Cory's life.

The Army determined later that the IED was a 500-pound force bomb, triggered by a pressure plate buried just far enough in the ground that a person's weight would set it off like a landmine.

CORY: Very instant. Very surreal.

The army evacuated Cory and his men to Kandahar, then to Bagram AFB. After emergency medical treatment, Cory was flown to Landstuhl Regional Medical Center in Germany. I flew in from the States to be with him. Cory's stepmother, Anne; his mother, Karen; her husband (Cory's stepfather), Ken; and my daughter, Shelby, who is today an air force nurse, also came. She told the family about CaringBridge, because the family member of a friend had used it. We knew we were going to be inundated with phone calls and we wanted to be in front of that, so we started Cory's CaringBridge site on day two to keep those who cared about Cory informed. As updates were posted, the phone calls dwindled, and all I could say was, "I guess this thing is working."

We tried to be as matter-of-fact as possible in Cory's journal, but on day three we laid it on the line. The doctors at Landstuhl told us that Cory had a depressed right-skull fracture, penetrating eye injury, collapsed lungs, burns, and more. He had several surgeries during his first week there, and it was touch-and-go. When a neurosurgeon tells you, "I've got to go back in and take some brain out," you sign the papers, hope for the best, and try to understand. We had to do that twice. The second time was on a Saturday. Some standby people were on the weekend staff. Cory's ICP—internal cranial pressure—peaked to the point it set off the alarms. The neurosurgeon was a contractor from Texas. He wore blue jeans, boots, and a big belt buckle. He said, "We're getting the surgical room ready and we're going in." I hit him with questions. I had been on Google researching brain injuries, trying to understand how what had happened to Cory would affect his life. The neurosurgeon listened for a moment while looking at me with a strange expression. Then he put his hand on my shoulder and very patiently said, "I'm trying to save your son's life." I tried to make light of it: "Don't take too many brain cells away from a Remsburg; we might be in trouble." Later, he came out of the operating room flashing a thumbs-up, and said, "I had to take out two different areas of the brain. It should have minimal negative impact."

The family went home on a commercial flight, and I traveled with Cory and a hundred or so other wounded warriors from Germany to the United States. The plane's interior was set up like a giant medevac, sectioned off for the wounded according to the level and intensity of their injuries. Those who could walk and talk and handle themselves sat in nylon jump seats along the walls. Some occupied gurneys lined up in the aisles, while flight medics, doctors, and nurses hovered and tended to them. Cory was the most seriously injured and he'd been set up off to the side near the back, on a specialized gurney, surrounded by medical equipment. Cory had his own doctor, his own nurse, his own respiratory technician. Their job was to care for him until he got to Bethesda Naval Hospital.

During the flight, I watched over Cory while the other passengers occasionally stared at me. Understandable. I was the only one in civilian clothes. I guess I must have seemed intensely preoccupied, because one of the loadmasters talked to the pilots—they were from the Louisiana National Guard—and they invited me to join them in the cockpit. I put on the flight headphones, and we talked about football, hunting, and fishing. They were kind.

The most seriously injured are loaded onto the plane last, which means that they're first to get off. At Andrews Air Force Base, the rear door swung down and an ambulance waiting for Cory whisked us away: Code 3—lights and siren.

Cory was in a coma, medically induced. Once the doctors at Bethesda Naval Hospital took him off the drugs, we just played the waiting game, riding the roller coaster of Cory's ups and downs as he fought for life and then slowly emerged into the real world. After three months, our patience and faith were rewarded.

President Barack Obama visited Bethesda while Cory was there, and he came to the ICU just to see our son and the medical staff! We were honored. Cory had met the president in France, before he was injured, and had pictures of that meeting on his hospital room walls. The president said he remembered Cory, and he signed those pictures and posed for additional photos with Cory, and then with Cory, Annie, Shelby, and Eric, Cory's brother-in-law. The president thanked Cory for his service and called him a hero. He acknowledged Cory as an Army Ranger and said that the Rangers were working very hard for our country. When asked how he was feeling, Cory gave President Obama a thumbs-up. The president shook everyone's hand, and Cory coined him (this time giving him an air force coin supplied by Eric). The president presented Cory with a presidential coin. Just before leaving, the president hugged Annie and thanked her again for Cory's service. President Obama also conveyed the First Lady's love and appreciation for Cory's service.

Any poly-trauma patient with devastating injuries and cognitive dysfunction has a long, tough road ahead. Cory has been no exception. My wife, Anne, and I wrote almost every day (at first), about Cory's day-by-day battle to get better, about the medical details, about his exercises, his travels, his visits from the family and from his Ranger buddies—and even his meals. Just in the past year, Cory began to help with the posts about his recuperation, the honors and appreciation he's received, and the relentless progress he's made with his nonstop therapies, including physical, occupational, and speech.

One hundred and nineteen days after the horrific events, Cory said his first word. He was in occupational therapy. His cousin Ed was watching. Manny, the therapist, asked Cory if he was getting tired, and Cory nodded in the affirmative. "Well then, *tell* me yes," Manny urged. Cory took a deep breath and said, "Yessss." Manny asked Ed if he'd heard that, and Ed had. The family was giddy with excitement.

At least that's what we posted in Cory's journal. But there's another story. My wife, Anne, was with Cory. He was learning about hygiene and brushing his teeth. Anne gave Cory some water, but it was too much and he swallowed it, gagged, and coughed. There followed a few choice words: "Are you trying to f****** choke me?" As word of Cory's vocalization spread, some of the families visiting other poly-trauma patients on the ward at the Tampa VA asked Anne if she could choke their kids so they'd start to talk too.

CORY: My daily routine: Get up, dress myself, eat breakfast, brush teeth, go to three hours of therapy—physical, speech, cognitive, memory, vision, occupational—eat lunch, go back to three hours of therapy, eat dinner, rest. Watch TV if there's time. Comedies. Jim Carrey, Will Ferrell. I'm learning to walk. And I take trips to become part of the community.

Our family draws strength from knowing that Cory gets great care. In the beginning he was never, ever without somebody from the immediate family by his side. Often I was that somebody, and when I went back to work, my wife left her job to become the full-time caregiver for a year and a half. That commitment allowed me to function.

The SOCOM—Special Operations Command—especially the Rangers, were all over us as well. They didn't forget. Never. To this day.

What I find absolutely amazing in all this is Cory's patience.

I didn't quite see that when he was growing up, or when he was in his early twenties and being deployed. But he has learned patience, and now no matter what he encounters these days, frustration is rarely on display. I've asked Cory how he does it. "What option do I have?" he says. He's right. He's got to deal with what he's got. One of Cory's big goals is to be independent, to walk, to talk more clearly, to drive. "What's wrong with living with your mother and father forever?" I've asked. His answer is always a cockeyed look: "All due respect, not my cup of tea." I'm certain this will come to pass. I'm a true believer in Cory, and he's never given me any reason to think otherwise.

CORY: I learned that if you are unhappy, you can do something about it. I discovered something I never knew about myself: my own strength. I never give up.

That's the Ranger attitude. Cory lives today at a rehab hospital in Pomona, California, but is by no means stuck there. We've traveled all across the country, from Phoenix to New York City, from Savannah to Saint Louis. He participates in Ranger activities and was recently promoted from staff sergeant to sergeant first class, attending the ceremony at the home base in Georgia.

Challenges remain. Cory's left arm is still totally paralyzed. He cannot use it from the shoulder down. It just hangs. If it doesn't get stretched, it crawls up to his chest. Through hard work, his right leg is at about 50 percent now, and he's begun to walk with a cane he someday hopes to abandon. Cory's right eye is unfortunately gone, but his vocal cords—which were literally bowed from the explosion—are steadily improving.

The Rangers investigate all explosions, fatalities, and injuries as standard operating procedure. As a family member I requested a copy of the investigation report and, with Cory, attended a briefing at Hunter Army Airfield in Savannah, Georgia. Cory had been out of the coma for about three months and was still a little hazy, but I believed it important for him to hear the story. The commanding officer, the field guys, and the enlisted folks who were in a leadership role went through a fifteen-page unclassified report that detailed everything that had happened on Cory's mission. The conclusion: Cory did his job as any Ranger would have, absolutely by the book. He couldn't have known about the IED. In fact, bomb-sniffing dogs on the mission had already canvassed that very area. Cory couldn't have done his job any other way.

CORY: I've never said, "If only." But I still feel kind of responsible. It's not the fact, just a feeling. Emotional support is available, other soldiers to talk to. Chaplains and the doctors.

Cory is a very compassionate man, very caring, but very pragmatic. He knows that there are risks attached to everything he—or any one of us—does. You hope everything goes right, but if it doesn't, you figure it out and keep going.

I've been asked more than once if Cory's injuries have made me angry. Absolutely not. I didn't get angry about the IED, I didn't get angry that the United States was in the Middle East. The government made the decision, and people like Cory and my daughter, and my other son—also in the military—understood.

No one would wish the challenges Cory faces on anyone, but I believe he had the maturity to handle it. That faith is reinforced by his attitude now, as well as on the day years ago that he called me, ready for his first deployment, and said, "If something happens to me, this is what I want done."

I've since taken that call many times, and I always prayed for the best. But through it all I knew that Cory was doing what he wanted to do.

> "From this day to the ending of the world,
>   But we in it shall be remembered—
>   We few, we happy few, we band of brothers;
>   For he to-day that sheds his blood with me
>   Shall be my brother; be he ne'er so vile,
>   This day shall gentle his condition;
>   And gentlemen in England now-a-bed
>   Shall think themselves accurs'd they were not here,
>   And hold their manhoods cheap whiles any speaks
>   That fought with us upon Saint Crispin's day."
>   —*William Shakespeare*, Henry V

MARGARET WORTHEN

In the Blink of an Eye

This is a story about a mother and a daughter and the love we have. I am amazed to be in the position to have to make decisions for my daughter, Margaret, just when she was about to begin her independent life. I am not sure how to communicate the process I've been going through as I attempt to take care of Margaret and also take care of myself. In part this is a mother's struggle not to give up her own life for the sake of caring for her child. I am struggling. I'm having a hard time coping with my feelings. I'm afraid. I'm sad. I'm trying to be positive and upbeat and energetic, but inside I am anything but that. I am having trouble seeing what is really going on because it hurts so much.

—Nancy Worthen, journal excerpt

I had been divorced for quite a few years and had been in a new relationship for about three. I lived in the same house in Richmond, Rhode Island, that Margaret and I had shared for twenty-two years. But I wanted to make a change, live closer to work in Providence, and not commute. I decided we'd let go of the house. Margaret would graduate from Smith College in May, and the house sale would close then, too.

On May 9, I left for a trip to Paris with a couple of girlfriends to have some fun. Margaret was at school, finishing her last paper. Afterward she'd come back to Rhode Island with her best friend and spend some time either in Richmond or at our beach house, which would one day be hers because it had been in the family since 1914. I planned to be back in time for her ceremony and the party to celebrate. After that, Margaret would start a job as a veterinary technician at the Animal Rescue League in South Kingstown. Everyone was excited.

The next day, Smith College tried to reach me, but I hadn't left information with anyone about where I'd be staying in Paris. The college tried an alternate number—my next-door neighbor—who called my ex-husband, Paul. Eventually the college reached one of my girlfriends, and she found me in Paris. Her news was direct: "Nancy, Margaret is in a coma. You have to come home now." I asked what had happened. She didn't know.

It took me almost a day to get back. I had to fly from Paris to London to get a direct flight to Boston. I was terrified. I thought Margaret had been in a car accident. I called the hospital from Heathrow, and the nurse said, "She's in surgery. They're breaking up the blood clot." I said, "Blood clot? What are you talking about? I don't know anything about that." The nurse said, "Oh my God, you didn't know? Margaret had a stroke." She kept apologizing for telling me over the phone, but I said, "Just tell me what happened." I started crying.

On May 10, at about three o'clock in the afternoon, Margaret had been in her dorm room, writing, when one of her friends heard strange gurgling noises coming from inside. She thought Margaret might be hiding an animal, and knocked on the door. She got no answer, but still heard the noises. The friend called other girls in the dorm for help. They tried to open the door, but couldn't. One of the girls looked under the door. She could see Margaret's hair on the floor.

Someone climbed on the roof and got into Margaret's room through the window. It looked like Margaret had fallen onto the floor from her desk beside the door, blocking it. She was having seizures. No one could ask her anything. No one had any idea what was happening.

Margaret was rushed to the local hospital in Northampton, Massachusetts. A CAT scan convinced the doctor that Margaret was in more serious trouble than they could handle. She would have been airlifted, but it was foggy, so an ambulance took her to Worcester, about an hour and a half away. Further testing revealed a blood clot in the basal artery of her brain stem.

Smith sent a car to bring Margaret's father, Paul, and her boyfriend to the hospital, where Paul signed for the surgery. Two of my girlfriends also went to Worcester to support Paul and be my surrogates.

Margaret was on the operating table by ten o'clock that night.

My boyfriend picked me up in Boston, and when I finally got to the hospital, the doctor told me that Margaret's prognosis was poor. He said that 95 percent of people with this sort of brain-stem stroke die, and the 5 percent who live stay in a vegetative state.

I broke away and found Margaret's room in the ICU. She was hooked up to a ventilator, and a feeding tube ran into her nose. A nurse said they were fearful about brain swelling after surgery and had to decide whether to drill a hole into Margaret's skull to relieve the swelling. Thankfully, that passed while I sat with Margaret and held her hand. I wanted some music in the room, soothing classical music, and someone made that happen.

I still can't find the words for how excruciating it was to see Margaret in that condition. I was in shock, trying to soothe my daughter and myself and not think horrible thoughts. Someone brought me food and tea. I got a prescription for Ambien. The college paid for a room for me at the family house near the hospital. A friend lined up people to stay with Margaret at night so that I could get some sleep, but I wouldn't let just anyone visit. One friend told me that she thought Margaret would die. I said, "No. Then you can't see Margaret, because you can't be thinking that when you're in the room with her. She's going to live. She's going to recover. She's going to be fine." I also didn't want visitors to talk like Margaret wasn't there with us. I assumed that she could hear and understand everything.

Three days later Margaret was out of the woods. Her brain wasn't going to swell, and she didn't have any infections. But she would die if I disconnected her breathing tube. The doctors wanted me to make a decision fairly quickly. I couldn't leave the tubes in her nose and throat because they would damage the sensitive passages. I could authorize a surgical procedure to put a feeding tube in her stomach, and perform a tracheostomy for the ventilator. If I did that, I would be saying, "We're going to keep her alive. We are not going to let her go."

The doctor said I should let her go. He said her chance of having any sort of life beyond a persistent vegetative state was terribly slim. I couldn't go with just one doctor's opinion, so I sought out several doctors and brought friends with me to witness and listen. My question was simple: "What would you do if this was your daughter?" But it was the wrong question. Unless it *was* their daughter, it was very hard even for a doctor to know what he or she would really do.

The answer was to talk with Margaret in my heart. She had written a paper on animal euthanasia, and believed that after a veterinarian first did everything to keep the animal alive, euthanasia was sometimes appropriate if a good quality of life wasn't possible. If that was what Margaret wanted for animals, it had to be what she'd want for herself. How could I not give her the chance that she would give to a sick animal?

I had her doctor read the essay. "But the paper is about animals," he said. "This is a totally different situation." I didn't see the difference. Short of having actually talked to Margaret about the decision, I believed she had written that fighting to preserve life is very, very important. Perhaps I just wanted confirmation of my own feelings, because I agreed. Not even doctors thought this a black-and-white decision. One neurologist said, "I've looked at her MRI and I believe it's possible that a connection still exists between Margaret's brain stem and her main brain, which remains totally intact. She has cognition, she just can't let us know." Even though Margaret was able to breathe some of the time on her own, I authorized a feeding tube and the tracheostomy.

The Glasgow Coma Scale is used to determine someone's consciousness. If totally unresponsive, they are in a coma. The next level up is minimally conscious, where the person can make some responses. Margaret wasn't brain dead. She wasn't in a vegetative state. She had all her reflexes. She flinched if pinched. She had a startle reflex. Her fingers didn't curl. She had some rigidity, but that relaxed over time. These were good signs. However, Margaret didn't open her eyes, follow voice commands, or seem to recognize people, although occasionally it appeared that she'd turn her head toward someone.

As Margaret stabilized, the hospital moved her from the ICU into a regular room. I had to find a rehabilitation facility next. I chose Spaulding Hospital, which came highly recommended and offered a special eight-week coma stimulation program.

Unfortunately, Margaret didn't make much progress at Spaulding, but she wasn't in a coma anymore, either. Her father and I believed that at *some* level Margaret was aware of our presence. We could see it. She would open one eye just a crack. It looked as if she might be tracking. Tears would run down her face at what seemed like appropriate times. When her father was particularly annoying, which was one of his character traits, she would get agitated and she looked like she was pissed off at her father.

But that would never happen when a doctor was around. She also never moved her eye up, down, side to side, or followed a pencil when asked. She could never squeeze anybody's hand. I couldn't tell if my hopeful instincts were real or magical thinking. I began to have doubts.

Too soon I had to move Margaret out of Spaulding. She'd have a few weeks of physical therapy and the therapist would say, "It seems like maybe she's moving her head," but then she wouldn't for a week. Medicaid doesn't pay for therapy if you can't progress, and if it's not paid for, no one will do it. I could have paid privately, but wasn't allowed to because the state ran the home and there were liability issues.

I had to try something new. I investigated electrical stimulation by electrodes implanted in the brain. I inquired about fMRI—functional magnetic resonance imaging—after I learned about a study in England. I researched so many possibilities, I no longer remember. Years passed with Margaret in various nursing homes.

Then I called a neurologist in Braintree, Massachusetts. His office said that he wasn't taking any more patients, but when I described Margaret's situation in an e-mail, to my surprise he agreed to an appointment. I shared all the avenues I had researched, and although he said he was open to trying things, he didn't hesitate to tell me when he thought some research was inconclusive. He did know the people conducting the fMRI study in New York, with Cornell and Columbia, and thought Margaret might be a good candidate because through the study we could finally, conclusively, know whether Margaret was minimally conscious or in a persistent vegetative state.

I remained hopeful and present with Margaret, thinking not about the past but about the future. I felt that she *was* there with me. I concentrated on my love for her and I felt her love for me. I guess I am an optimist, and I tried to use anything to help me be my best self. I practiced gratitude every day. *What can I be grateful for right now? I'm having a cup of tea and I love the taste of tea in my mouth.* The simplest thing. If I could feel that gratitude, I could get through the day. I had practiced meditation, the Buddhist idea of breathing and staying in the moment, and I did that, too. *Right this moment, I'm with Margaret. Right this moment, I'm at work. Right this moment, I'm sleeping.* Anything was better than allowing my mind to conjure either the worst or the best scenario, because those weren't real and I didn't know what was. The whole Buddhist philosophy is to have a don't-know mind. Who am I? I don't know. Why is this happening? I don't know. Then you don't try to find out. Not that I wasn't madly doing research and learning everything I could, but I also had to understand that I was the mother, not the doctor. Not a neurologist. I had to trust my instincts. I had to trust someone to help me.

Help came. Sometimes I asked for it and sometimes not. I hardly thought about food, but my boyfriend cooked for me on the weekend and he'd leave enough in the refrigerator for the week. Months earlier, when my house sale closed and I was in Boston with Margaret, my friends packed my kitchen and bathroom, moved the boxes, and unpacked everything at my new home. It was amazing.

I was able to get Margaret into the fMRI program, but we had to delay her participation for months because she got pneumonia several times. Her tracheostomy tube had long been removed, but at one point it needed to be hooked up again in order to clear her lungs. At first I didn't want to do that, because it seemed like such a large step backward. I even considered letting the pneumonia take her, because her quality of life was awful, but I didn't.

In New York, at the fMRI program, the medical-ethics doctor asked me, "What will happen if you find out that Margaret's in a persistent vegetative state? How will that change your idea of what should be done with her?" I said, "I don't know, but it certainly will change if I know for sure." Then he flipped the question. "What would you want for Margaret if you knew that she was conscious?" I said, "Communication. If she can make her wants and needs known, it would make her life meaningful."

Dr. Nicholas Schiff ran the project. He did a regular MRI and a PET scan and told me that Margaret's main brain worked.

There was no atrophy. Electrical charges functioned normally. "Margaret is totally present," he told me. "She is thinking. She is here. She is conscious. There is no question in my mind."

No doctor had ever been so definite before. Dr. Schiff showed me the MRI and the PET scans. "This brain is not dead. It's not in a vegetative state." I had no words, but I was thrilled. Now, if what I'd always believed was true, we had to find a way to communication.

Dr. Schiff asked a nurse to open Margaret's eyes. He held his driver's license in front of her face and asked Margaret to look at it. She did, with her left eye. Then he asked her to follow it when he moved it up and down. She did. She could both hear and track. I got so excited. I said, "Dr. Schiff, you're amazing. Margaret is amazing!"

Margaret could only use her left eye and she found it easier to move it down than up, so Dr. Schiff told her that down would mean "Yes." He asked, "Is your name Margaret?" Yes. "Is your father's name James?" No. "Is your father's name Paul?" Yes. Simple questions to which we and Margaret knew the answers. She got seven out of ten correct, a very accurate confirmation that she was indeed there. Witnessing everything were Margaret's father and a few other medical professionals.

Now my heart was in my mouth. I was stunned. I should have cried, but I was too happy for tears. Dr. Schiff sent Margaret back to her room to rest, promising to try again soon.

The next time, Dr. Schiff left Margaret's eye closed and asked me to stand a bit away from her but in her line of sight. He opened her eye and asked, "Can you see your mother?" Yes. *Then* I cried. Everyone cried. Not only did I know that Margaret was there, she knew I was here.

That evening a visiting friend from college, who had walked

into that emotional scene, took me to an expensive club for drinks. I was so delirious that I told everyone within earshot, "My daughter, she talked to me. She knows I'm present!" They had no idea what I was going on about, but I didn't care. I wanted to toast everyone.

To this day, no one knows why Margaret had the stroke. She didn't have any medical history that indicated a potential. She didn't have high cholesterol, didn't smoke, didn't drink, wasn't overweight. The only possible factor is that she was taking birth control pills, but it's impossible to definitely make the connection.

Margaret knows she's in a hospital. She knows she had a stroke. She knows that she has severe limitations. But she doesn't grasp the concept of years having gone by. I avoid some information. I've never asked Margaret if she'd been aware and listening the whole time since the stroke. And I've never asked her if she wants to live. If she said no, I don't know what I would do.

I *have* asked, "Are you sad?" No. "Are you discouraged?" No. "Are you happy?" Yes. She laughs now. And she cries. She has two more ways to show her feelings.

For six and a half years, Margaret has been relatively peaceful. Maybe it's because her body is quite relaxed and she never had painful tremors, or her arms tight against her body. She can get angry and frustrated, and then her whole body will get tense, her legs will straighten and her arms will shake—and she might even make a sound. When we don't know what these movements mean, we ask, "Are you in pain?" No. "Are you uncomfortable?" Yes. If she says she's in pain, we try to find out where. The questioner's skill is very important.

As soon as she was finished with the Cornell study, she also got speech therapy to use her eye—which has to be held open—in conversation. That went on for several years. We had a whiteboard and would write questions so that she could read.

Margaret keeps making progress. It's not very fast, but it's moving forward. She has a computer now. It needs to be programmed with pictures/choices on which she can focus her eye, and it will "speak" preprogrammed sentences. But there are limitations, because no professional has time to thoroughly program the machine.

My job as a caregiver is to be creative and use what I know about Margaret to introduce her to whatever gives her life meaning. Some activities work better than others. We went to the movies, but we couldn't talk about it afterward. I could ask her, "Did you like it?" Yes. But I can't ask, "What did you think of *The Dark Knight?*" She can't answer that kind of question. I raised money for a van in which to take her places I thought might interest her, but she drew the line at going to her high school reunion.

For four years I had a meditation group that met at her facility and she sat in. Now I'm having an art therapist work with us. Margaret likes it. She laughs and is excited. I guide her hand—it's me painting for her—but what's beautiful is that she has the experience of moving her hand and seeing her hand cre-

ate a color and an image on the page. *She is creating something.*
If she thinks about moving her hand, it's the same to her brain
as if she's actually doing it. The more she can do that, the more
it stimulates her brain. I want her to move her hand on her own
one day, so I'm doing everything I can.

Today I live about forty-five minutes away from Margaret. I
see her three times a week. Her father sees her three times a
week, too. She lives in Massachusetts because the MassHealth
state insurance program is far superior to the health care program in Rhode Island. MassHealth covers people with acquired
brain injuries to help them live in the community. Margaret has
qualified. I'm moving her into a house with four other disabled
adults so that she can have a more normal life. There's a dining
room and a kitchen. Some of her roommates might be able to
cook. She can have visitors. She'll be part of something more like
what a twenty-eight-year-old would be doing, living on her own.

I am always hopeful. I continue to investigate other paths to
communication. I'm closely in touch with two projects, at Brown
and at Harvard, that use electrical brain implants to help minimally conscious and locked-in patients to communicate.

I'm so happy that Margaret is now in the world. Between my research and her artwork, people have been able to connect more
easily with her. She has a life. It's a small life, but it's still a life.
A small life is not nothing.

There is also terrible loss along the way—beyond what happened to Margaret. Her boyfriend loved her madly. He came to
see her every week for three years after the stroke. Then he realized that the life they had talked about would never be possible.

I'll never have that son-in-law or grandchildren, since Margaret is my only child. There is no one else after her.

Today I accept Margaret the way she is. I only ask myself what I can do to make her life better. Her room is beautiful. Her surroundings are beautiful. Her clothes are clean. She has wonderful, kind, and generous caregivers. She has a massage therapist who loves her and talks with her. She has an art therapist. She has a devoted father who plays music and reads stories to her. She has me.

So in the end, this story of loss is also a story of living. We are together. She knows it. This is her life, our lives, now.

December 25, 2012:
This holiday season has been blessed with some wonderful things for Maggie. She has spoken a few words: "Okay," "It's hot," and "I'm fine." She was answering questions from her caregivers. This holiday season has been blessed with some wonderful things.

—journal excerpt

Caregivers Need Care Too

The job of a caregiver is usually thrust upon us unexpectedly. It can involve the loss of friends and free time, and trigger feelings of isolation. To counteract these issues, reach out to friends and family members and utilize Internet tools to solicit help with tasks. It is not selfish or a sign of weakness to call on professionals and others around you to provide support. No one should shoulder the caregiving load alone, and yet many try to do just that.

Today there are many resources for caregivers.

Consider joining a support group. The National Family Caregivers Association (nfcacares.org) and Today's Caregiver (caregiver.com) offer multiple ways to connect with other caregivers. Attend a meeting near you and assess the dynamics of the group, the quality of the leader, and most importantly, how you feel during and after the meeting.

Ask for help from relatives and friends. It is also helpful to reach out to members of your church, synagogue, or other place of worship. Consider starting a CaringBridge online SupportPlanner. The calendar helps you coordinate care and ask for help with daily tasks.

Remember that it is essential to take care of yourself as well as your loved one. Give yourself permission to relax, enjoy, and not be a caregiver for designated periods of time during the week. Schedule time on your calendar for you. You have earned it.

TOM TOWLE

Heartfelt

TOM: While playing catch with my son, he threw a ball over my head and I had to run after it. I was surprised to feel sharp chest pains. I was thirty-seven, didn't smoke, and was in good condition. I'd never had any health problems beyond having my tonsils out. But you can't be too careful, so I went to the doctor. He wasn't my regular guy, but I knew him and trusted him. I got an EKG, and he said, "You don't have enough signs of anything." The diagnosis: indigestion. I got some Maalox, and he told me to come back if the pain didn't go away.

A week later I was in the emergency room with a heart attack.

MICHELE: A few months earlier, my doctor thought I had ovarian cancer.

TOM: The doctor had told me that he was 90 percent sure it was cancerous and severe enough that Michele wouldn't be around for very long. I never told Michele, but the doctor had said, "You'd better get your things in order." It turned out to be a precancerous tumor, but it was wrapped around everything and took four months and two operations to get it all out.

MICHELE: Tom likes to joke that it scared him so much that he had a heart attack. It's as if we took turns getting sick.

TOM: When the heart attack happened, my first thoughts were about Michele and the kids, Sara, Molly, and Tom Jr., who were then only four, five, and six. What if she'd have to raise them alone? I had life insurance, so I wasn't concerned about money in case I died. But I told Michele, "I'm going to make it. Don't worry about it." I wanted her to stay upbeat. My regular doctor encouraged me, too. "We can fix this," he said.

At first he tried an angioplasty, but six months later he said, "Let's open up your chest." He did a double bypass, and I came out fine. I exercised more and stayed in damn good shape. I could work. My career was growing. It took me about a year to get back on my feet, but life got back to normal.

MICHELE: I had a bachelor's degree for teaching but no license, so I went back to school. Now I teach full-time. We lived in a nice home, and the kids went to private school. Life was really good until Tom's job started to go bad. He was down a lot of the time, which was rough on our marriage. We struggled financially and had to move. But Tom managed to get back on his feet, and I worked and I earned my master's degree. One day, Tom came home from work and said, "I lost my job." Then things went from bad to worse. I was diagnosed with MS and a month later Tom had another heart attack. It was just nuts.

TOM: I thought it was my second heart attack, but the doctor told me it was my third. I'd had a "silent" heart attack earlier, and they found the additional damage during my tests. It didn't knock me out, but this third attack put me in the hospital, where I got a pacemaker. The stress had started getting to me. I would be doing well and *boom*, I'd get knocked back two or three steps. After my first heart attack I figured maybe I could get another thirty-five years, but after three, I felt that time was running out too early. I had all the usual fears about dying. I'd have a twinge in my toe and think, *Oh my God, my heart's doing something.* I felt bad, because it's not great for kids to realize that Dad is vulnerable and frail.

I went to the mortuary, planned my funeral, and picked out the casket. I even gave the funeral director a photograph that I wanted to be used in the obituary. I told no one.

MICHELE: In September 2011, Tom went to the doctor because he was having chest pains, but didn't tell me. I found out because I ran into his doctor at daily Mass, and he said, "Do you want to come by and see the results of Tom's stress test and echo?" That was news to me. He said Tom hadn't had a heart attack but that something called the "ejection fraction" was so bad that he recommended we introduce ourselves at various hospitals to talk about a heart transplant.

TOM: I like to get all the facts before I talk about something that could make the family freak out. Better to find out the results of the tests first, rather than tell them I might have a problem, get tested, and have everyone go crazy waiting two weeks for the results.

MICHELE: We took the doctor's advice and in November we went to Abbott Northwestern. The kids came, too. Now they were grown. Molly is a nurse, Tommy is a paramedic. Sara is in marketing.

The doctors said that if we got into the program, we and their group would be connected for the rest of Tom's life. They sincerely wanted to be there for us. We liked that approach. They explained that Tom would have to go through a huge battery of tests because they didn't give hearts to just anyone. They asked Tom, "Do you want to do this?"

TOM: The doctor didn't say I *should* have a heart transplant, but the team at Abbott Northwestern gave me the odds of how long I would live without one: two to three years, tops.

MOLLY: Actually, the doctor said, "Either you do nothing and see how long you can maintain where you're at without any new symptoms. Or you can go ahead and get a Left Ventricular Assist Device right now. Or you can try to get a transplant." Dad wasn't thrilled with the idea of an LVAD, which involved a lot of equipment to wear and carry around, and I don't blame him, so he said, "I'd like to move forward with the transplant."

When Dad left the room to get a lab drawn, the doctor told our mother, "The minute he has any new symptoms, pack a bag. He'll be staying here." Dad was in Class IV heart failure.

TOMMY: Dad had very little heart function left, but he had lived with it for so long, and was otherwise healthy, that nothing ever seemed like an acute change, so no one noticed. His body simply compensated and acclimated to his heart disease. During his tests I remember him saying, "That stress test seemed fine. I don't feel like I got too short of breath." But when the numbers came back, they were far worse than the doctors had expected. Outwardly he looked like his heart was working at 30 to 40 percent of normal. In fact, it was only 10 to 15 percent.

TOM: I agreed to start the process. What else can you say at that point?

MICHELE: Once Tom made the decision and did the tests, he suddenly decided he wanted to go to Charleston, South Carolina. We had a great time; however I noticed he looked pale and had increased shortness of breath. He also had hardly any appetite. I'd be hungry and he'd say, "Aren't you full?" Tom could hardly walk off the Jetway at the airport when we got home. I wouldn't let him touch a suitcase at baggage claim. We went to the hospital the next day for tests, and the doctor said his blood pressure had dropped and that he'd been experiencing abdominal angina. "You're at the end stage of heart failure," he said. "You don't even have enough blood to digest your food. That's why you felt so full all the time."

TOM: When I ate—say a bowl of soup—I felt like I'd had Thanksgiving dinner. In Charleston I went to see the aircraft carrier USS *Yorktown* alone. Walking out on the long pier, I had to stop four times. On the ship, with the stairs and gangways, I couldn't go fifty feet without stopping. I was so tired. I waited with some elderly and handicapped people for a ride off the pier, but no one came, and I had to walk back. It took me half an hour to walk less than five hundred feet. I realized then that I'd have to get the transplant.

SARA: Dad was admitted to Abbott on December 7. Relatives found out, and we kept getting phone calls, so we set up the CaringBridge site and sent out an e-mail with a link. I'd had a friend in college who was in a horrible accident and was paralyzed and brain-damaged. He had a site. I liked that the CaringBridge pages were ours. We could pick the background and write our own story. It became an information tool and a sounding board. I got a CaringBridge app for my cell phone. I could check in every day, or hour, or minute—and update when needed.

MICHELE: Even though Tom was in the hospital, he kept getting worse. I spent lots of time with my landline phone on one ear and my cell phone on the other. Then I got my cell bill: $476. I told Sara, "I want to write on the CaringBridge site. There's no other way to do this."

SARA: It was perfect for sharing information when family came in from out of town. People could show support or share love or ask questions. We created a community, and it helped all of us.

TOM: When Michele started posting, she got very philosophical about life and her feelings. She did some wonderful writing.

TOMMY: No one in Mom's or Dad's family really understood how sick Dad was. I don't think I or my sisters did either until he had to spend two weeks in the ICU.

SARA: Transplants are complicated. You can't be too sick to get one. To keep Dad's heart from failing even more, he got the Left Ventricular Assist Device as a bridge to keep him alive and make the rest of his body healthier for a potential transplant. The implantation operation required three weeks of inpatient recovery and three months of home recovery. You can't accept a heart until the placement procedure is healed. Then you're on the list for three months.

TOM: There are different priority classifications. Priority 1A is the top. You get to be on that list for thirty days, during which you're hoping and hoping for the right donor heart to come along. Weekends are the best for transplants, because that's when accidents happen—someone on a motorcycle gets killed—or a patient is surrounded by her family and disconnected from life support. Even if you're not at the top of the list, if a heart comes in that fits your specifications, you can get it. But the odds are different.

I was at the top, and nothing came along. On day twenty-nine Michele and I were sitting on our patio and I said, "Well, I don't think it's going to happen." I was okay with that. The pump was working and I felt well. Some people get the pump and wear them for the rest of their lives. There are batteries, and cords. When I traveled, I had to pull a rolling, milk-crate-sized thing through the airport scanners. On many occasions the TSA were all over me, hand-patting me, saying, "Come over here and leave your bag over there." I'd say, "I can't. I'm attached to it." They're a pain, but if you're alive instead of dead, I guess it's worth the hassle and pain.

MICHELE: Tommy was able to live with us, and the girls would take turns helping me at home. All three were fantastic. We met a neighbor who said his wife had had a heart transplant a year earlier and he gave us her hospital bed to use. The kids helped settle my nerves, because it was scary to have someone around who lived on batteries. I told Tom he had to live by the rules, and that if he was a bad boy, I'd take his batteries away.

TOM: When I posted on CaringBridge, I'd sign as "Battery Boy." Humor, the Towle way.

MICHELE: A few months after Tom got his pump, he suddenly told me I had to drive him to the hospital. An alarm had gone off, and the unit went into backup mode, which gave him about thirty minutes to live. At Abbott, they found a crack in one of the pump lines, and they had to send out for a new controller. As a result, Tom got lucky and was upgraded to a 1A category, with priority, for a transplant.

Almost a month later I came home from morning Mass to find Tom shaking and dry-heaving and white as a ghost. He could barely speak. He said his head was spinning. I thought he'd had a stroke. He'd managed to call the hospital and they were waiting for us to arrive.

Tom had an infection at the exit site of the drive line to the pump. He got antibiotics and a room for ten days. Further tests revealed a blood clot inside his pump, in addition to the infection. He needed a transplant soon or he'd have to get another pump, which meant more recovery time off the list.

I was mad, sad, scared, nervous. I didn't want to see Tom go through another surgery. Of course, like most husbands he took it in stride and didn't want us to worry. I had begun to hate the pump, but tried to remember that he was still alive because of it—and the great heart team at Abbott. But the little glitches along the way were driving me crazy.

No heart became available, so Tom needed a new pump. "It will be a simple surgery, just a couple hours," the surgeon said. The kids and I kissed Tom good-bye at 6:30 a.m. He told us he loved us and said he'd see us on the other side.

Three hours went by. Four. Then the doctor came out and said he wanted to talk to me and the children only. He said Tom had lost a great deal of blood. They were putting in another pump. "We'll know in an hour if he's going to make it," he said, then left.

MOLLY: He said it was between Tom and God. My mom had an anxiety attack. They gave her Ativan. We were all sobbing. Every one of my dad's siblings had come in from out of town. There was nothing we could do but pray. Most of us thought he was going to die. I tried to tell myself that if, God forbid, it happened, it would be okay. He'd had a good life. Mom could live with us.

MICHELE: The surgery went on for nine hours. We said a Hail Mary every five minutes. Tom went through fifty units of blood. It was just awful. My brother-in-law is a doctor and he told me Tom would die. I said, "No, you don't know Tom. He's gonna be okay."

SARA: I didn't think Dad would die when they started the surgery. It was supposed to be quick; go in through his abdomen and switch out the pump. But then a doctor came out and said, "Well, Tom's giving us a little trouble in there. We're having to shock his heart."

At six or seven hours another doctor came out and said, "It's really dicey in there. It's not going well." They had to open up his whole chest again to repair a leaking artery.

TOM: The surgeon removed the original pump, put me on bypass, and replaced it with a different model. It didn't work. My pressures wouldn't normalize and they couldn't close the wound, due to bleeding and inflammation. They decided to try another model.

I only found out about this afterward, of course, mostly from reading the CaringBridge journal. I was amazed at what the doctors managed to do. I felt love for my family and guilt at what I'd put them through. I had the easy part. They went through the emotional drama.

When the hospital threw a going-away party for the surgeon who did my pump surgeries, he asked me, "How did you handle all that? Did you think you were going to die?" I said, "No." He said, "How can that be? You had a failed pump, you're waiting for a transplant, you go into surgery, you kiss your wife good-bye. You *don't* think that you may die?" I said, "After over twenty years of having heart attacks, stents, IPVs, LVADS, whatever—I came out of it every time. What just happened was another step. I'll be out of here and be back to myself in however long it takes to recover."

MICHELE: Tom came home three weeks later, in early July. He continued to heal, to do cardiac rehab, to hope for a transplant. In September he began his month at priority 1A, and we went about our lives, hoping, while waiting for the phone to ring. On September 26, just a few days before Tom would have been downgraded to Priority 1B, the transplant coordinator at Abbott called to say they had a likely match.

SARA: We all went down to Abbott and waited through the night for confirmation on the donor heart. Everything looked positive. If it stayed that way, Dad would go into the operating room at 8:00 a.m., be put under at 9:00 a.m. and get out of surgery in four to six hours.

We announced the heart on CaringBridge and updated frequently. We got back support and prayers. Dad seemed calm as we all waited for the morning.

The heart arrived on time and in good condition. The doctors put Dad on bypass and took out his LVAD and his old heart.

At 1:30 p.m. his new heart, a *young* heart, was in—and beating!

TOM: Since the surgery I've had two serious rejection episodes, but they just pounded me with medications and did biopsies to monitor everything. The biopsies are like an angiogram. They go up into your carotid artery, wind it around going to the right ventricle. They grab five tissue samples and then they come out. They don't knock you out for it, they just give you the happy juice. It takes fifteen minutes. The scale is: zero you're okay, three you're going to die. I just had a biopsy yesterday and it was a zero, and I've had three zeroes in a row. Before that I had a two. The biopsy schedule is one a week for four weeks, then every two weeks, then every month, then every three months. After a year you go back every six months.

The biggest thing I've taken away from all of this, besides a new heart, is that I wouldn't have made it without my family, and I don't think my family would've made it without CaringBridge. Everything I've read on the site has humbled me. I had no idea the joy I brought to those who loved me. CaringBridge allowed my family to work through difficult emotions. Michele has said that being able to express her feelings helped her to put events into perspective—especially with the responses she got in return. The love, the care, it comes back to you, fills you, and, like a strong heart, keeps you going.

"As a social worker I'm happy when people confide their innermost feelings to me. It's part of why I do what I do. I'm there to listen and help them focus on their goals. I want to hear what they're afraid of, their concerns, whatever they're angry about. It makes me feel good when I've established a rapport and they feel comfortable with me. And yet, I have had great difficulty talking about my own health issues and journey with cancer, because I am usually the caretaker and am not comfortable being the one taken care of. My cancer taught me a big lesson. It's a humbling experience. You're not in control anymore. Physically, I needed help. At work, I needed help. At home, I needed help. You have to rely on others. So it's okay to ask for help. It's okay to let people be there for you. Allowing people to be helpful is a gift to the caretaker as well. Accept the gift—and never give up."

—*Amy Albien, colon cancer survivor*

CRYSTAL AND CRAIG HEWITT

Part of God's Plan

People have always asked us, "How can y'all put a smile on every day? How can y'all keep going? How can y'all keep living like you are?" And every day we have to decide: Today is a new day; God has made this day for us and we are going to live it. We have totally depended on Him.

—Crystal Hewitt

CRAIG: Crystal and I lived right through the woods from one another. We went to the same elementary, middle, and high schools, and we had mutual friends. We didn't start dating until we were in college, after Crystal stopped being preoccupied with other boyfriends, and we discovered that we shared beliefs, morals, and values. We got married when we were twenty-one. Parker was born soon after, and then Haley. We cherished family and wanted to grow in our relationship with each other and with God, and to raise our kids to follow Christ and to love others. Crystal taught preschool at our church. We couldn't have been happier.

One summer day a few years ago, Crystal took Parker, who was five, and Haley, who was three, in our Honda van to pick blueberries like they often did.

CRYSTAL: I was stopped, with my signal on, about to turn into a driveway. I looked in the rearview mirror, at the kids in their car seats, and said, "Guys, guess what? We're almost there! Are y'all so excited?!" Then I saw this big truck coming up behind me really fast. I thought, *Oh my gosh, this truck has got to stop.* The driver tried, but there was not enough road left. The truck hit a man on a motorcycle behind me. I saw both the man and the bike fly up in the air. And then I felt everything crushing down on me. Glass popped. Metal crunched. I screamed, "Parker! Haley!" They didn't answer.

After that I kept slipping in and out of consciousness, as if sleeping and waking up from a bad dream, and sleeping again. I was still in what was left of our van. Someone tried to push an oxygen mask toward me. I could only move one arm and I kept swatting it away, saying. "Leave me alone! Get my kids. Don't deal with me, get my kids."

I woke up again when they started to cut me out of the van. I said, "I can't breathe. I can't do it anymore." I shut my eyes, prayed for Craig and prayed for the kids, and got ready to die. I thought that was it, but soon I was in a helicopter. I woke up in a hospital room and saw a nurse by my bed. I hurt all over, but I asked her, "Where are my kids?" She wouldn't answer. I said, "Please get my husband in here. Nobody's telling me anything. Where are my kids?" The nurse left and I could tell by the horrified look on her face that she didn't want to come back. I must have passed out again, and then Craig was right beside the bed. He wasn't alone. I saw our pastor and my mom and dad, and I knew something was no good. I felt sick, like I was drowning, like the bed had turned to quicksand. Craig looked into my eyes and put his arms over me, and said, "It's okay." Then he said, "They didn't make it."

CRAIG: The accident happened off of Highway 6, down toward the Lexington/Red Bank area in South Carolina. The closest hospital was in Columbia, but the ER was full, so the helicopter took Crystal to Medical College of Georgia, in Augusta, an hour away. I got the phone call at work as I was about to head out for lunch. Someone from the ER told me that Crystal had been involved in an accident and that our two kids did not make it. I kept thinking that couldn't have been right. That's not how they're supposed to deliver that kind of news.

I knew I couldn't drive. I was a nervous wreck. I called my parents, in-laws, pastor, anybody I could, and finally got a ride. I'm sure we broke the speed limit the whole way, but the trip seemed like it took forever. All I could do was pray that what I'd been told was not true. But as soon as I walked into Crystal's hospital room, she asked where the kids were. Telling her was so hard, but I did, and then held her.

CRYSTAL: I have never felt such unbearable pain. We had lost everything. And then I remembered God. From the beginning of this nightmare we relied on Him every minute. We prayed together and totally trusted that our kids' dying was probably not His perfect plan. No, it was more the Devil saying, "Hey, you know what? I'm gonna take her kids and she's going to fall on her face. She's going to go *away* from God." But I have not. We have only grown in our faith for Him, because He is all we had to lean on. We wouldn't allow the Devil to take our joy of living for Him. We've had to struggle every day, but every day we focus on God.

CRAIG: Losing our kids turned our world upside down.

We've endured a mountain of pain and will never know why. But we cling to knowing in our hearts that God saved Parker and Haley from any hurt and suffering, and received them in Heaven. Crystal and my earthly journeys will continue on until God calls us home to be with our kids. God is in total control! We walk by faith and not by sight! We thank God for allowing us to be Parker and Haley's parents. I thank Him for the most beautiful, caring, loving wife in the world, and for saving her. I almost lost Crystal. The doctor said that if the truck that fell on top of the van had squeezed her a millimeter more, she'd have been paralyzed.

CRYSTAL: Today I look back and wonder how in the world Craig and I ever kept going. I'm a mommy who lost two children. He's a daddy. How could we get out of bed? How could I make breakfast like it was just another regular day? How could he go to work? But somehow we also feel a great peace that goes beyond words, and maybe understanding. I only know it's an incredible experience to have Him hold my hand over and over again. I'd never seen a double rainbow before, but now I've seen so many that I believe God is sending them from Parker and Haley to tell us, "I've got them. Y'all just keep on, because they're waiting for you up here with me." It comforts us to know we will see them again. Otherwise, this life plain-out sucks. It's full of hurt and grief. Everyone goes through losing someone. We're not special. But losing your children I would never wish on my worst enemy. It's horrible. I can't imagine handling something like this without having God, without having that faith to turn to, without having Him be your strength to help you every day.

CRAIG: After the accident, Crystal had back surgery. She had to have a "turtle" cast around her whole midsection. She did physical and occupational therapy. We also started seeing a counselor, who was very good at explaining things and motivating us. When we didn't want to do anything but lie around and hurt and miss our kids, she said that you can only get so many days off from work for grieving. Then you have to go back to the real world, back to doing your job, back to life. So we did that.

We worked with our counselor for a few years, three times a week—though we feel like she's still part of the family. We'd schedule appointments for the morning just so we had a reason, an obligation, to get out of bed. Crystal did the same with her physical therapy, so that she started the day right and didn't just get sucked off into the grief.

We felt so much better every time we met with the counselor. We did more than talk and unburden ourselves. She set minigoals to make sure we did activities, like have lunch together, before going back home. We did everything we could to avoid the depression. She'd let us know that the way we felt, whatever we felt, was okay. Everybody grieves differently. She explained the road map of grief, where you can go, and what turns you don't want to take.

It really helped that a friend of ours started a CaringBridge site for Crystal, and kept everyone updated. Soon I started posting, and eventually Crystal did too. CaringBridge brought such comfort, especially when Crystal left the hospital and we started going back to church. We dreaded the, "Oh my goodness, how are you?" and, "How's your back?" questions. But we didn't get them. Everybody in our community had already read Caring-Bridge. We didn't need to go into the same story every time we bumped into someone. They already knew. Instead, we gladly embraced their hugs.

CRYSTAL: We went shopping after I got home, and in a parking lot we saw a mom trying to get her three kids into her van.

Craig and I looked at each other and we knew that we wanted to run up to her and say, "Cherish every minute you have with your children." Craig and I poured our life into our kids every day. We rarely left them with anyone, because we wanted to be together all of the time. We have so many awesome memories, and every day something reminded us of them, and we shared them on our journal.

We thought all the attention would eventually stop, but it's been more than three years since the accident and people are *still* asking about us, *still* following our CaringBridge site. We could be in Walmart getting groceries and a stranger will walk up and say, "Y'all are the Hewitts. We've been praying for you." They reach out. They start crying. Parker and Haley's passing still affects our community—and it's spread.

The CaringBridge community has become our family, in a way. We feel like all these people are walking the journey with us. I believe I could call any one of them on the phone. Or, when we're having a hard day, write it in the journal to let people know that they can make it through their troubles, too. It feels really good to know that everybody is listening to us.

CRAIG: It's a miracle to me. Our counselor once said that it's typically unheard of for people to be that emotionally attached to a story and still talk about it so long after it happened. There's only one way to explain why: God is definitely using our circumstance.

CRYSTAL: When the hospital discharged me, I wasn't nearly ready to go home. I couldn't be where Parker and Haley had lived, see their rooms, touch their things, stand in the emptiness. Craig understood, and my parents let us use their lake house, which we started calling our Retreat Home. But a retreat from one thing didn't let me retreat from everything. I couldn't sleep at night. I was scared of the dark. Many nights we would cry ourselves to sleep, thinking that what had happened could not be right. I had to have Craig with me everywhere. Because of the turtle-shell case I could hardly walk. Craig had to help me in and out of a wheelchair, and help me to use the bathroom.

Craig went to our real home and that was okay. He could do it. He fed Parker's fish, got our mail, sometimes brought back little things of Parker's and Haley's. I knew we had to go back, so we took baby steps. Some days we'd drive by, and the closer we got, the more I'd feel like I was about to come out of my feet. I could barely handle it. My heart beat so fast. More than once I yelled, "Hit the gas! Hit the gas!" But soon, because of counseling, I was able to stop in front of the house and sit there for a few minutes, until I started to squirm and cry.

The first time I was able to go inside wasn't planned. We'd pulled up in front, sat there as usual, and I said, "What the heck. Let's try to go in." Craig said, "Are you serious?" I said yes, and he knew to stop asking questions. We went inside, but I could stay for only a few minutes, and only downstairs.

One day our counselor told me, "You're scared to go into a room by yourself because you feel like a lion is going to jump out at you." I agreed, and she said I just had to tackle it. So Craig would stand outside the bathroom door and I would go in by myself just to use the bathroom. I'd sit there, scared out of my mind, but saying, "There is not anything that's going to happen. I am in the bathroom. I am safe. God is with me. I am okay." I just had to tackle it. Eventually it got better and better, and the lion went away. I could walk all the way to the bathroom by myself, use the bathroom, wash my hands, and come back out without Craig being there.

CRAIG: As a husband I wanted to make everything better

right away, but I could only do that if I could bring Parker and Haley back. Instead, I prayed over what I could do, how could I take the right direction as head of our household? How could I lead our family, help Crystal, be strong myself? Again, our counselor helped me to understand that men and women process grief differently. Crystal never liked hearing, "Everything's going to be okay. Don't cry." It was better to just console and love her and let her be as emotional as she needed instead of trying to get her mind off the subject with a false sense that everything would be all right. I also struggled with emotions and the opposite idea: that I'm not supposed to be upset. It was okay for me to be upset, to be vulnerable and show my emotions. As I was there for her, Crystal was there for me. We became each other's crutches, and for whatever reason, both of us were never down at the same time. One could always be strong and hold the other up.

And yet each day we go through seems to get harder and harder. You would think that it would get easier as time goes on, but that is not the case yet. Parker and Haley have been in our thoughts constantly, especially on their birthdays. Haley could never decide what she wanted to do for hers, except that she wanted the whole family to get together. I wish we could have another birthday party with Haley by our sides. I can see her now trying to blow out the candles while trying not to spit all over the cake. She was the most adorable little girl ever. Such a little princess, and a daddy's girl for sure! I'm glad Parker was with Haley for her birthday, holding her hand, giving her a hug and kiss from us. He probably helped her cut a big piece of cake and eat it too. He helped her open gifts and play with her new toys. I'm pretty sure Jesus also had a special present waiting for Haley. I wonder what it was? I pray that she wrapped her arms around Him and thanked Him so much for everything He blessed her with.

CRYSTAL: At Christmastime, the year of the accident, Craig's gift to me was a framed art piece that read, "Our family is a circle of Strength and Love...Founded on Faith...Joined in Love...Kept by God...Forever Together." It was awesome, because "together forever" is what we've always said to each other since we began dating. We knew it from the beginning and still say, "Together forever, I love you."

We have two more children now. Our daughter is Ellington and our son's name is Emerson. Ellington just took her first steps a few weeks ago. That's amazing, because she was born with spina bifida. She had surgery when she came out of the womb and had a shunt put in her head. The doctors said that she would be in a wheelchair for life and would not be able to walk. They were wrong. She looks and acts like an absolutely normal two-year-old. She walks normally. She speaks normally. The occupational therapist sees her every three months and is about to drop her because she's met all of her goals. When we found out about the spina bifida, we were prepared to deal with whatever God laid upon us. But we knew that there was no way that God would give us a child I couldn't lift with my injured back, or take care of. No way. We trusted God, and He blew us away. He knocked the socks off the doctors.

Ellington and Emerson smile so much it's contagious. I feel like Ellington knows Parker and Haley, too. We talk about them and show them pictures, and we'll tell them the story as they grow up. We even have a little card that Craig made with a picture of Parker and Haley on one side and Ellington on the other, because we'll be out somewhere with the children and be asked by complete strangers, "Oh, are these your only two kids?" We give them the card as an easy way to say, "No, they're not. This is Parker and Haley. I'd love for you to read our story on Caring-

Bridge." Sometimes Ellington points at the picture of Haley and says, "Hay-eh." She points at Parker and says, "Park." She knows exactly who they are. I'm excited for her to get older and hear more stories about them.

CRAIG: We're very open with the life that God's laid out before us, and if people have questions, it's easier to give them the card directing them to CaringBridge. I'm a full-time photographer now—families, kids, weddings, whatever—and because many of my clients know what we've been through, they use me, because they understand how we value family.

CRYSTAL: As far as we've come, for a long time I was afraid that while I was knocked out in the van, maybe my kids were crying out for me. What if I could've done something but didn't hear them?

CRAIG: A good friend from church came by a few months after the accident and shared a story that helped us a lot. Her little daughter was really good friends with Parker. We always said that they would get married one day because we all got along so well and had the same beliefs and morals. She said, "I was waiting for the right time to tell y'all, but I really want to share this. After the accident I had a dream that was so real. I saw your van all crushed. You were inside the van, and Jesus stood outside, holding Parker's and Haley's hands. Parker looked up at Jesus and said, 'But Jesus, what about Mommy?' And Jesus said, 'Mommy's got to stay here to take care of Daddy.' And Parker said, 'Okay.' They were holding Jesus's hand and they were totally fine. They weren't hurting. They weren't in that van, they were outside that van with Jesus. They weren't suffering."

Comforting Words for Those Who Have Lost a Loved One

Even the most well-spoken among us often struggle to find the right words to say when someone dies. The American Cancer Society and the American Hospice Foundation offer these suggestions:

Acknowledge the loss, and use the word *died* to show that you are open to talking about how the person really feels and you don't expect him to put on a brave front: *"I heard that your_____ died."*

Express concern: *"I'm sorry to hear that this happened to you."*

Be genuine in your communication and don't hide your feelings: *"I'm not sure what to say, but I want you to know I care."*

Offer support: *"Tell me what I can do for you."* Or pitch in without waiting for a request.

Don't assume you know how the bereaved person feels; ask: *"How are you feeling?"* or *"Do you want to talk about how you are feeling?"*

Avoid sayings like, "It's part of God's plan" or "He's in a better place now" unless you are very familiar with the person's faith.

Give space to the grief. It's not helpful to remind the person of the bright side during this dark time, or push them to move on with life. Everyone progresses at his or her own pace.

AARON HOLM

Wiggle Your Toes

I was forty-one years old and a regional manager for a firm that placed information-technology consultants in projects at companies like Target, Honeywell, and 3M. If a company decided to change software and needed temporary staff to put it in place, I would find it for them.

It was my first day back after the Christmas and New Year's holidays when I'd taken a couple weeks off to be with my family. I had arrived early and was catching up with one of my recruiters when one of my administrative technicians, Buffy, called. She was running late because she had a flat tire on I-394, a busy highway that is a main corridor into downtown Minneapolis. Buffy said a tow truck was on the way and it wasn't a big deal. I told her to be safe, and we hung up.

A short while later, Buffy called again and said the tow truck couldn't make it for a few hours. She was four months pregnant, it was January, and it was Minnesota cold. I decided I'd get her out of there.

I found Buffy's car pulled over on the shoulder well off the highway, and could see the back right tire was flat. I was wearing a business suit and had not come intending to change a tire, but I'd done it lots of times in college. I figured I could probably change it in ten minutes if she had a good spare. I had the flat tire off and was putting it in the trunk of her car, when I was struck from behind.

The driver was an elderly gentleman traveling about fifty-five miles an hour on the shoulder. He had merged onto the highway from an on-ramp a mile away and never realized that he was on the shoulder. He was just a confused driver. Never saw me. Never hit his brakes. The car smashed into me, right at my knees. Imagine standing behind a car and having another one crush you between bumper and bumper.

I was alert and conscious the entire time, but Buffy went into shock and wasn't capable of doing anything except scream. I pleaded with her to settle down: "Hand me your phone so I can call nine-one-one." I could see it clenched in her hand, but she was frozen in place.

I needed help badly. I was in pretty rough shape. I tried to stand up. I tried to move myself to the shoulder of the highway, because I was hidden by the cars—kind of in between Buffy's car and the car that hit me—and people driving down the highway couldn't see me. Instead, cars flew by at fifty miles an hour, kicking debris from the accident into my face. I was afraid that another car or a semi would come flying up behind me and take me out. It wasn't a great situation. I knew I was in big trouble, but I also knew I was alive, and that kept the adrenaline going and put me into survival mode.

Somebody finally stopped and called 911, but she didn't report the accident the way she should have. The police didn't realize it was an injury accident until they arrived at the scene.

A cop covered me up with a blanket because I was cold. The

police photographer took pictures of me. Finally, an ambulance was called. I don't remember the pain hitting me until the ambulance got there and the EMTs started moving me around. Until then I think the adrenaline had taken over the pain and, during all the waiting, allowed me to think clearly. I wondered if I was ever going to walk again. I knew one of my legs was gone. It wasn't severed, but my foot was up at my hip. That kind of position led me to believe my leg wasn't going to be mine anymore. It was pretty ugly to look at, and my other leg was all twisted up and not much better.

The ambulance took me to North Memorial Medical Center, where I was stabilized and got a heavy dose of morphine. The pain vanished. All of a sudden I was pain free. A buddy of mine walked into the emergency room, and I joked, "Bob, we're going to have to cancel that tee time." That was my immediate mindset: *I'm alive, I'm in the hospital, I've got good care, let's figure it out.*

―――――――――――――

There were procedures I didn't know about, some of which gave me a good laugh. A nurse would wake me at 4:00 a.m. for a blood pressure check and meds. I had no idea I had to state my name and birthday before getting the medication. The first time, I was sound asleep, dopey, and in a strange bed. It took me a while to figure out who I was and when I was born. By that time I was wide awake.

One day my wife brought me some T-shirts. We unhooked the IV so I could slip off the old one and put on the new one. But afterward we forgot to rehook up the IV. I went without it for about three hours, until the medical professionals discovered my misbehavior. From then on, Amanda and I promised not to play doctor anymore—at the hospital; I know what you're thinking.

Sometimes the morphine monster would sneak into my room and I'd hallucinate a bit. Once, I asked Amanda why they were shooting off fireworks outside my window. Whew! If I'd had a Grateful Dead CD that day, I would have worn it out. I had to write to friends who might have visited that day to explain my silliness.

As you can tell, I never wasted a moment asking, "Why me?" This is the hand I've been dealt. It's a pretty crazy hand for a person who's been fortunate his entire life and never had anything bad happen, but it is what it is. In fact, since then I've often told people that it was easier for me to cope with my injuries as the victim than if it had happened to my father, my wife, or one of my children. I thought about them throughout. I knew I had to be cool and confident so that they would be cool and confident. If I was a mess, they'd be a mess. I needed to direct and control myself, because everything I did and said would have a tidal-wave effect on the people who surrounded me and whom I needed the most to help me get back to the new normal. So I went into management mode just like I did at the office, and I told them, "We've got work to do here. I can't do it on my feet, but you can, and I need your help." I've got good friends I can count on. We all banded together and decided to educate ourselves about what I needed to keep moving.

I've never been shy about asking for help. I don't consider myself a very smart guy. To compensate, I surround myself with knowledgeable people so that as a group we can do terrific things. If I need something, I'll ask for it and get it. The accident proved to me that I had surrounded myself with good people.

That might seem like a strange attitude to some, but I have always considered myself a go-getter, a thinker, a planner. Maybe an over-the-top planner, if you ask my wife, Amanda. I want to know where we're going, what we're doing, what's around us when we get there, how to maximize the trip. On our honeymoon, my wife was poolside with a book while I was scuba diving, renting a Jet Ski, meeting people in the bar and exploring. I just don't like to sit still.

Within a day or two of the accident, we talked to a contractor, and he went to work on the house within the week. We remodeled the kitchen, the doorways, the entire upper floor of our bedroom, and my bathroom. That tells you a lot about how we mobilized and went to work. I meet people every day who have suffered similar injuries and who have spent three or four months in the hospital and are about to be released but haven't even thought about making modifications to the house.

We also had visits with attorneys and with practitioners who specialize in prosthetics. We found that Ottobock, a world leader in prosthetics, had their North American headquarters in Minneapolis. I called them to ask a salesperson to come to my hospital room. "This isn't anything we've done," they said. "We don't go to hospitals. Practitioners buy our products." I said, "I don't care. If you can come up, we would appreciate it. I want to talk to you about your product. I want to meet somebody who's wearing a prosthetic, and I want to talk to every practitioner in town who has fit your product."

My family never told me to slow down. Instead, we put together project groups, and I considered myself the project manager. We had one group looking at transportation. I talked to my company about workers' compensation and about equipping my office so that if I came back in a wheelchair, I could get into my office and behind my desk. We put together the top fifteen or twenty things that needed to be done in the next thirty, sixty, and ninety days, and then set out to do it.

Within a couple of days, I could move myself from my bed into a wheelchair. I actually snuck out of my room and into physical therapy because I knew some kind of exercise would help my mind and body move forward. Lying idle was killing me more than anything. Before the accident, I cut wood with a chain saw in my backyard. I was active with the kids outside. I played sports. I was in pretty good shape, but I knew my upper body needed to be stronger than it ever had been because I was going to be relying on it for the short and long term. I had three kids under nine years old at the time, and they certainly weren't slowing down. I knew I had to catch up.

There were probably some down times, some depression. The hardest part was coming to grips with the fact that my kids were going to see me like this, and I'd have to explain it to them. When my kids came to visit me in the hospital for the first time, I was very strong while they were in the room, but I broke down when they left. The story was tough to tell. They're great kids, smart kids, and they were happy that Dad was alive after an accident, but accidents, to kids, are terrible things. My wife told me many times that they'd break down together, that they'd cry when she tucked them in at night. But I realized that they just wanted to be with their dad, and that gave me a lot of strength. I assured them that things were going to be good. Things were going to be the same. It was just going to take Dad a little time to get back on his new feet.

After six surgeries and eighteen days of recovery I got out of the hospital, but I lost both legs above the knee.

I never went after the other driver. His air bag had deployed on contact. He had been hospitalized and released the same day. The local police department tried to prosecute him—they wanted to put him in jail—but they called me the day before the trial and I said, "Absolutely not." There was no reason to do that. They talked about making him do community service, and I said, "If he was confused driving, why would you give him some other responsibility?" I didn't ever want the guy to drive again, which he probably hasn't, but I forgave him. I knew it wouldn't help me in any way, shape, or form to see him put away.

I also declined to attend the court hearings. I didn't see any value in that, and it didn't fit into my plan of moving forward. I cut the cord and never followed up with who he was or what happened to him. I moved *forward*.

My wife is the real trouper. Our marriage is as strong as ever. Soon after I finally got home from the hospital, after the kids went to sleep, I asked her how she was doing. I called it a sanity check. She said, "As long as you are doing well, I am doing well." That was about the most satisfying answer she could have given me.

After the accident her phone rang off the hook. Everybody wanted to know everything. One of the things I tell people now is that when one of their family members has a traumatic experience, call the cell phone company and get the unlimited plan. Her cell phone bill was about $300 that first month.

CaringBridge turned out to be a lifesaver. My great friend Bob, an IT guy, set me up with a laptop and introduced me to CaringBridge after he learned about it from the hospital. We got hundreds of hits every day. We tried to post two or three times a day to settle down the calls, keep people assured that things were going to be okay, and let them know how they could help.

People I hadn't talked to in many years wrote in the guest book. I joke that I've led several lives, because I grew up in one community, Saint Paul, moved over to White Bear Lake and picked up a bunch of new friends, and then went off to college in southern Minnesota and picked up a bunch of friends there. I had all these pockets of people, but you know how it is. You get married and start having kids and you lose track of a lot of them. As word got out, everyone funneled to CaringBridge, and it served as the most phenomenal tool you could imagine to keep everyone informed that I was going to be okay, was optimistic, and had the support I needed.

I was very surprised at the outpouring of support. There were strangers and people from all over. One time I wrote about phantom pains and how they were affecting me. Someone wrote back that their neighbor was a physical therapist who had recommended a solution, which helped, so CaringBridge was a tool both for communication and for gathering resources for healing. One of the EMTs who picked me up off the pavement wrote to me on CaringBridge and said, "It's so nice to know how you're doing. We never get to hear about the victims."

Once home, I hit the physical therapy hard. I needed to improve my upper-body strength. I got a wheelchair and learned how to use it, while my doctors made sure my skin grafts healed and I had no infections in preparation for prosthetics. The doctors did an excellent job, and I would be able to distribute my weight in multiple areas of the prosthetic, which would make it easier for me to manipulate the legs.

Because of the war in Iraq, prosthetic legs were in high demand and there was a long wait. But the increased demand also meant that companies were investing more research and development into creating a highly sophisticated product. Prosthetics used to be much less complex. For decades, those who needed a prosthetic were typically elderly patients who were suffering from complications due to diabetes. Today the recipients are more likely to be young and healthy. The legs I ordered had a built-in microprocessor, which meant the prosthesis could memorize the way I move, dance, moonwalk, or do back flips.

Before my legs came, I had to see my plastic surgeon—a phrase I never thought I'd say at my age. When I left his office, I had a few more stitches in my left leg. A part of my leg hadn't healed properly, so we removed it. I called that the Tony Soprano mode of recovery. If it doesn't work, get rid of it.

Outside of the healing process, having our prosthetist fit me for "shrinkers" was the first major step toward being fitted with prosthetics. Shrinkers are tight socks used to form, by compression, the ends of my legs in preparation for the prosthetics. Two additional layers, each one a bit more constrictive, were placed over the socks. They took some getting used to.

I also had a good conversation with my prosthetist about what to expect: a lot of tripping and falling. "They're not magic legs," he said.

Eventually my computerized legs—C-legs—arrived. Wearing a test socket, which made me a little over four feet tall, I was able to stand and walk again. A week later I put on the finished product. It was great to be five foot ten again.

Of course, the real fun was learning to walk again. It took a lot of trial and error. At one point I asked my prosthetist for a key to his training facility, as I thought I might have to move in. Slowly but surely I learned to walk again, dealing with tenderness and other issues along the way, moving ahead step by step. In the end it was like riding a bike. Once you get it down, it becomes second nature.

My wife and I had talked a lot about what I might do next. She was working as a project manager for Target in Minneapolis and had taken a leave of absence after I was injured. After I got back to work, she extended the leave, because she was my legs. The local press had picked up on the accident, and we started getting even more phone calls and e-mails. People whose brother had been in a motorcycle accident or whose father had diabetes, all of whom had lost a limb, wanted to know where I had gone for physical therapy, what kind of leg I was using, what I did for phantom pains. Since I like to talk to people and I knew there was no resource for that kind of information, I fielded phone calls and visited people in the hospital. One day I called my wife from work and said, "We need to create an organization." I knew from CaringBridge that a website would be very important, that people could use it as a first resource and us as a second resource.

Eventually Amanda resigned from Target and was very involved in creating our organization, as were a lot of my friends who helped me along this journey. I asked some of my colleagues at work if they wanted to be part of the board when I got it going, and they said, "Absolutely. It's awesome to see you recovered with the resources we've been able to provide. Let's give those resources to other people."

The name of the organization is Wiggle Your Toes. It came from our CaringBridge journal when I wrote about the phantom pains I experienced and my anxiety about a surgery that had been scheduled for the following day to resurface my femur and get it ready for prosthetics. My doctor had told me, "This is the big one." I wrote about how I could still feel my toes and felt I could still wiggle them. I wrote, "Do me a favor: Wiggle your toes for me." People picked up on that and had T-shirts and sweatshirts made with Wiggle Your Toes on them. One guy and his wife were down in Florida for spring break and wrote that when they left, their friends said, "Good-bye," and he replied, "Wiggle your toes!"

We thought it sounded weird and that some people would look at us funny. But I also thought the novelty would help us get noticed. It has.

Prosthetics is a science and an art, and it's engineering. If the right person isn't putting you back together, it's not going to work. I've got legs that cost $40,000 apiece. They're computerized, with built-in microprocessors. I charge them every night. But if the part that fits to your body doesn't match up 100 percent, the prosthetic itself is worthless. It has to fit absolutely perfectly or it won't work. It's all alignment, just like building a house. If the foundation is off, so is the rest of the house.

Tillges Certified Orthotic Prosthetic has clinics throughout Minnesota and western Wisconsin. I was a patient there for about two years. I finally resigned from the IT consulting firm to get Wiggle Your Toes going as a nonprofit, and was going to Tillges for adjustments and upgrades. I would ask about the business and whether they'd tried different things, such as building a database of information about patients so the staff doesn't have to ask the same questions every visit. The owner of Tillges took notice and started courting me, trying to get me to come to work for him. "Absolutely not," I said, "I know nothing about your business or insurance or regulations." It was out of my wheelhouse. But after several more conversations with him I knew I'd meet a lot of people and that it tied into what I wanted to do, which was give back to the limb-loss community, help people out, make sure they're working with the right people. So I gave it a shot, and now I work for the company that put me back together.

I've met other people who've lost both legs above the knee like I have, and that's as disabled as you get. I wouldn't be walking right now without the technology that I discovered. There aren't a lot of people who lose both legs above the knee and walk again, because it is such a difficult and complicated rehab.

I try to wear shorts when I walk into a hospital room, because right away the person I'm coming to visit will think, "Whoa! I thought *I* was in rough shape! Look at this guy." But sometimes I go to the hospital right after work, when I'm still wearing long pants. I'll sit and talk with the person for fifteen or so minutes, and I can tell that they don't believe they'll be able to walk again. They'll say, "Yeah, that's what the doctors and nurses are saying, but how the hell do they know? They've never lost a leg. It's more complicated than what they're telling me." Then I'll lift up my pants legs and say, "You can do it if you want to. From what I've learned by talking to you for fifteen minutes, you're capable of doing it. Here's proof right here that it's possible." The conversation changes. Optimism is created.

The best thing for anyone who's suffered a limb loss is to see me.

In the end, I became the guy *I* wanted to see when I was in the hospital. I went above and beyond personally, and it stuck. People wanted to be part of that. They saw success, and everybody wants to be part of success.

I joke now that my wife still thinks golf is rehab, so I get to play a lot. I'm playing twenty to thirty rounds a year now, which is a lot for me. Before the accident I played maybe five rounds a year, because we were raising kids and that took priority. It took me a couple of years to get back into shooting in the 80s, but I shot several rounds there this year and am hoping to break the 70s within the next couple of years.

Passionate people and phenomenal technology are out there to help anybody who has suffered the loss of a limb get back to doing what they like to do. They just have to make it work. I'm here to help.

> "Man often becomes what he believes himself to be. If I keep on saying to myself that I cannot do a certain thing, it is possible that I may end by really becoming incapable of doing it. On the contrary, if I have the belief that I can do it, I shall surely acquire the capacity to do it even if I may not have it at the beginning."
> —*Mahatma Gandhi*

SALLY DALY

We Were Just People

I met Devon in a creative writing class at the University of North Dakota during the fall semester of my second year and his third. I was nineteen and he was twenty-two. My first memory of him is when he came to class at the beginning of the year with a gigantic black eye. It was the biggest, purplest black eye I'd ever seen. Everyone asked, "What the hell happened to you, man? Were you in a fight?" He said he'd gotten elbowed in the face in a rugby game. He loved rugby.

I found out later that the black eye was how he discovered his tumor.

Devon didn't ask me out until December. He had to critique my terrible poetry for our class, but he also left a Post-it note on my stuff that read, "Hey, we might be having a party. You should give me a call." He left his phone number. I called immediately. He told me then, and often, that I was beautiful and smart. It was truly love at first sight, we were together ever since, and it was easy. I still have that Post-it.

Devon was hilarious. A character. A presence. You knew when he was around, because he always had something to say, something to make you laugh. His whole body would take on a persona. He had red hair and a red beard and a really deep voice, which he used to do pretty much any accent requested of him: Irish, Scottish, George W. Bush. Whenever I felt down, he'd pull out a character and make me laugh from the bottom of my gut. I'd had relationships that weren't much fun, but everything with Devon was fun. He shared a house with four other rugby guys, and they loved to dress up crazy and have theme socials with other rugby teams. My college life was never boring again.

Devon also liked to tell me that I kept his life together. We complemented each other pretty well. He'd keep me laughing and I'd keep him focused.

I found out about Devon's tumor by accident. He was on the phone with his mom and getting more and more agitated: "Yes, Mom, I know.... Okay, Mom! Okay." After he hung up I asked what was going on. He said, "My mom doesn't want me to play rugby."

"Why not? It's so fun."

"It's because... You remember I had that black eye?" Then he told me about a kiwi-sized tumor in the left side of his brain. He'd never felt any ill effects. "But when I went to the ER for a CT scan of my injury, they said, 'Your face looks good—but you have a massive tumor in your brain.'"

I didn't know how to react. I think I said, "Oh. Well, that's probably a good reason not to play rugby anymore." But I noticed right away that I didn't feel like I wanted to run screaming in the opposite direction. Later some people close to me said, "You know, you don't have to do this. You don't have to stick around." I did, though. I had to. I wanted to. The tumor wasn't a deal breaker for me. I didn't get angry or resentful that Devon had waited nearly two months to tell me, because his reticence had allowed me to fall in love with him because of who he was, not out of pity. And by then we were already very close. We knew there was more between us than just dating. I think we both knew very early on that one day we would marry each other.

I knew privately that Devon struggled with things, but when he shared with other people, he would sometimes put on an act. He would make jokes about it to break the tension. I was the one who saw him falling apart in the car after having too many drinks. I had just turned twenty, my boyfriend had a serious tumor, and I only wanted to comfort the big strong man with the big red beard when he sobbed because he was terrified of what might happen when he had surgery.

Devon went to Duke Medical Center in Raleigh-Durham, North Carolina, to get the tumor removed. His mom, Kathy, found out about CaringBridge and started a site for him. I went to Raleigh-Durham as well, and later I read the first guest-book entries, looking for my name. I was hardly mentioned at all. I was just "the girlfriend," sitting there through all of it with my boyfriend's family, feeling like there was no one supporting me.

On the site, Devon made light of everything. Humor was his coping mechanism, and mine as well. Early on he wrote, "I'm going to be checking into the hospital in about an hour, and then you guys get to listen to my mum. I get blood drawn today, along with the ever-popular urine sample, and some X-rays. I'm going to grab a bite to eat here, and then I am looking forward to a gown, cold hands, and the fabulous dining provided by hospitals nationwide."

Devon made it through the surgery with flying colors. The tumor was located in the language center of his brain, so partway through surgery they brought him out of sedation to have him speak. He answered questions in both English and German (his college major) to be sure that removing the tumor wasn't causing extra problems. Later, he wrote, "Today, while getting my bandages changed, I got to look at the cut itself. My goodness, it's like a massive worm on the side of my face. It's going to look awesome!" Later, he decided he was tired of having a lopsided haircut, so he made me shave his head with his beard trimmer in the bathroom of our hotel. "I got a Mohawk. It actually looks decent. I still don't know how many screws I've got in my skull, but Sally counted forty-seven stitches on my face."

The pathology results showed that Devon had a Stage III tumor, so he had to have radiation, and then chemo for at least a year, plus monitoring and regular MRIs. That didn't seem to bother him as much as not being able to play rugby in the fall, but he could still coach. "If I don't actually practice with the guys, then I'll just yell at them and condition them until they are Greek gods of stamina," he wrote.

During the next few years, we were just people. We weren't people with cancer. We finished college and traveled the world when we could. I moved back to Minnesota from North Dakota, and Devon was going to follow me as soon as he finished school to become a teacher. I needed a job and worked for Barnes & Noble until, on a website for nonprofits, I saw a listing for Caring-Bridge. I didn't know CaringBridge was founded by someone who lived in my hometown. The office was five miles from where I grew up. I used to play soccer across the street.

I applied for a customer service position. I did a few interviews and was hired. Now I've been with CaringBridge for two years, and love my job.

Devon and I finally got married. Because of Devon's original Post-it to me, which I'd saved, we continued the theme and had people leave messages on Post-its in our wedding guest book. We moved into a one-bedroom apartment. He looked for a teaching job, and we talked about one day buying a house. We wanted to start a family in the summer. Meanwhile, Devon religiously got follow-up MRIs every three months in the first year after his operation, then every six months, then every eight months, then every year. The scans always came back perfect. With each passing MRI we felt like we were getting a lot closer to the magical five-year date. If you make it that long without new cancer, you're good.

Devon wasn't totally issue free. Because of the operation and the hole in his brain where the original tumor had been, he had seizures and had to take medication. The seizures didn't happen often, just often enough to be annoying. He lost his driver's license once, but was told that if he didn't have any seizures for a specific amount of time, he could have it back. We'd get within days of the date, and he'd have another seizure. "Dammit!"

Devon experienced a few other changes, which seemed minor.

His reaction times got slower. When we played board games, he took longer and longer to decide on his next move. Then all of a sudden, after he finished his student-teaching requirement, it was tough for him to read out loud. We saw doctors and they chalked it up to a med change.

But we never talked about what would happen if the cancer came back. His tests were clean, and we had no reason to believe it wasn't gone. We were young. We'd only been married for six months. We were going to be together for years. We had tons of time.

I worked the morning that we had our annual appointment to have his MRI read, then I went home and picked him up. I walked into the house saying, "Okay, let's go! Let's get out the door!" He just sat on the bed, staring, saying nothing.

I asked what was wrong. He said, "I'm really scared."

"I am, too. This will be five years. I'm nervous, but excited. Let's just get this behind us."

"No, I'm scared it's going to come back," he said.

I understood, but I still thought he had nothing to worry about. I tried to reassure him. "You know what? If it comes back, it won't be like last time. It'll be this tiny little pipsqueak and we'll be able to shoot it out with a laser, and it won't be a big deal."

Part of me now thinks that Devon knew it was back, but didn't want to say so.

On the MRI of Devon's original tumor you could see that it was about the size of a kiwi, or an egg. It took up less than a third of one-half of his brain. The latest MRI showed a tumor that took up pretty much the entire left side of his brain. Compared to a clean scan a year earlier, the difference was devastating. His tumor was back, and was much, much worse.

On the scan, the neuro-oncologist with the Minneapolis Clinic of Neurology showed us the two blood vessels that run down the middle of your brain—dark, long, skinny lines that should be parallel to each other. In Devon's head, the line on the left side was shrunken and pushed aside. The tumor was growing and trying to get to the right side of his brain. Another MRI only two days later showed even more growth. It was scary how quickly it grew. The look on the doctor's face was clear: he'd tried everything he could for us, but the tumor was infinitely bigger, and nothing could be done.

When Devon saw the MRI, he looked the doctor in the eyes and just flat-out said, "So, I'm dying?" I don't remember the doctor's reply, only that it was clinical and direct. I was blown away, and I tuned out. Then the doctor said, "I'm not comfortable sending you home for the weekend"—it was a Thursday night—"but if you want to go home, you can." He walked to the door. "I'll give you guys some time," he said, and left the room.

We cried. We hugged. We cried. We kept crying. Finally, I asked Devon if we should call his dad.

"Probably should," he whispered. Afterward, he checked into the hospital, and the next morning, we were back on the Caring-Bridge site. But this time I did all the writing. I signed on my first time as, "Hello all, wife here." What an odd feeling. Then I brought everyone up-to-date on the terrible news.

Despite what seemed like a hopeless situation, the doctors decided to have some surgeons look at Devon's MRI for additional opinions. Maybe something could be done. He certainly couldn't continue with that thing in his head. But the news was bad. "We can't do it," both said. "If we do, we'll just aggravate the tumor, speed up the process."

I still don't know where I found any strength at all. Maybe from the family. Everyone was there, filling up the visitors' room. But I was in shock, a whole different kind of shock, half-conscious, just moving automatically, like a zombie. I knew that if I stopped to think about what was happening, the pain would be unbearable.

It had taken only a couple of days to realize that we were never going to take Devon home, and our focus shifted to making sure he was comfortable and not in pain.

Devon was pretty pissed off. He knew what was happening, but the doctors put him on several drugs, and after that he was never the same. One time, in the ICU, he looked at my older brother and said, "Hey! You! Quit stealing from children."

As we were wondering what that meant, he said, "I want to get out of this fucking place." That we understood.

Devon wavered between being groggy, telling me he loved me, and struggling not to die. We figured out that one reason he wanted to hold on strong was to wait for his brother, Ian, to arrive. When Ian got here, all of the Dalys were able to spend some precious time together as a family. He heard from us all how much we admired his strength, how proud of him we were, how much we loved him.

Everyone was so generous and gave me what seemed an eternity alone with my Devon. During this time, he spoke to me with ease. He did not stumble upon words, nor did he hold back in sharing his love for me and his deepest feelings regarding what he was facing. He was wise, comforting, and beyond profound. If there was ever a doubt in my mind about what happens next in life, my Devon showed me that there is no reason to be afraid.

Our families went home to rest, but Ian and I stayed to make sure that Devon was free from pain and discomfort. We made Devon comfortable together, and together we were able to ease his passing. Devon went quickly, in my arms. His strong body took some time to understand that Devon no longer remained. Devon did not suffer.

Afterward, my in-laws asked me if Devon had said anything to me before he died that might have comforted and inspired me. I told them that at one point he'd looked me straight in the eyes with a very concerned face and said, "I have this dream that you are sleeping and you can't wake up. I can't wake you. Why can't you wake up? I'm going somewhere else. I'm floating and getting bigger and bigger, and you're getting smaller and smaller and smaller." He also told me that I would be okay and that I had to keep living life. And he asked me for forgiveness. I said, "Babe, there is nothing to forgive. If you need forgiveness, you have it."

That was just a few hours before the end, and I don't know where that came from. He had been monosyllabic the whole day.

After Devon passed, some people said, "You guys lived such a normal life." I would say, "Yeah, because we didn't even consider the option that this thing was going to come back so soon." We just did our thing. We were just people. We weren't going to let cancer run our lives.

Before Devon was buried, I slipped a secret note, on a Post-it, into the suit jacket I had my dad give to the funeral director.

It's interesting that I ended up working at CaringBridge, but I discovered that a lot of the people who work there are drawn to it because they've used it, or they've had a family member who had a site. I can't imagine a more supportive place for someone like me, someone who's lost her husband. Everyone was following my posts, so they knew exactly where I was at when I came back to work. If I have difficult moments, they cut me slack because they understand.

I'm still writing on Devon's site, though I don't know how long I'll go on. Right now I want to put out there what I'm going through and get back the support that fills the guest book. People write, "That's okay," "Thanks for sharing," "We're with you." As a widow I need that. I was amazed to see how many people cared about Devon and me and our family.

Otherwise, I am still lost, but putting things back together. I did not cut ties with Devon's family. There's no way I could do that. They're my family, too. Sometimes I think it would be easier to just go my own way, but it *wouldn't* be easier. I loved Devon and I love them, too.

I do have to move on, though. I had really long hair when Devon and I got married. He always loved my hair. A month after he died I chopped it off into a bob, in defiance. It will grow back eventually. I recently bought a motorcycle, a Honda Rebel 450, and my short hair is easier to tuck up under my helmet. My dad rides a Gold Wing and my older brother rides my dad's old Honda. I'd always wanted to have a motorcycle, and then I fell in love with a man with a brain tumor and a seizure disorder, and I let go of that dream. Now I realize it was just postponed, so I reclaimed it. Last summer I put over four thousand miles on the bike. I ride it every day. In the beginning it took all of my concentration, so I didn't have space to think about Devon, or the fact that I'd lost him and how crappy life can be sometimes. Now, when I feel overwhelmed or I'm thinking too hard about stuff, I can go for a ride and clear my head. It's a huge relief for me. But it's also weird not to think about Devon. I can't help feeling a little guilty afterward.

My story isn't over yet. I don't have any grand advice for healing or how those in similar situations can move forward, because I'm still in it. I just have to live every day. That's progress for me, because not too long ago I had to work to get through each minute. Getting through a whole day is a giant step.

They say that you sometimes see the person you lost in your dreams. I did once. In my dream, Devon and I were at a party and we both knew that once the party was over, we wouldn't be together anymore. I dream of having him here still. Just a regular life with Devon.

Tips for Caregivers

Being a caregiver can be as exhausting as being the patient, yet a caregiver is more likely to feel guilty about asking for help or for a break from responsibilities. If you are a caregiver, or know someone who is, here are a few suggestions to ease the load.

- Find time to laugh—With all the heavy responsibilities and decisions a caregiver must make, comic relief is an essential component of coping. Laughter reduces stress hormones, such as cortisol, epinephrine, adrenaline, and dopamine. Try a funny movie or even an audiobook of great jokes or anecdotes.
- Ask for help—Caring for someone is a huge responsibility and is often more than a one-person job. It is important you don't overwork yourself. Ask a friend, family member, work or church group to help you when needed. Be clear and concise about what you need.
- Give yourself a break—Caregivers, more than anyone, deserve it. Always make sure to set aside time to relax. Taking time out to enjoy your favorite activities, or even talk to a trusted confidant, can help relieve stress and reduce its negative effects.
- Tap into your faith community—One powerful way of receiving support is to write a letter to your faith community asking them to pray for the person who is ill, and also for you as a caregiver.

ALEX FEINE

Fighting Fire with Desire

SUZY FEINE: On a Friday night, in the middle of August, when nothing much was going on, my husband, Dan; our son, Alex; his girlfriend, Hannah; and I had collected green branches from all over our three-acre property and piled them into a bathtub-sized fire pit behind the house. We typically burned them using gasoline. I told Alex, "I'm going to light it up and get rid of it." He said, "I'll grab some gas and come out with you."

Alex filled a water bottle with gasoline and sprinkled some at one end of the pile. I lit it. Alex walked to the other side of the pit, about four feet away from the blaze. He lifted his arm to pour on more fuel so I could light that side, and as he tipped the bottle sideways, the fumes caught on fire and the bottle exploded, drenching his shirt.

I jerked my head up at the sound. Alex was blue from his waist to his neck, engulfed in flames.

We're all taught that when you catch fire the best reaction is to stop, drop, and roll. Instead, as do 95 percent of people covered with flames, Alex ran. We live out in the country with no fences, so there was nothing to stop him. I chased him, screaming, "Stop! Drop! Roll!" but Alex was one of the fastest kids on the track team, and I had no chance of catching him. He couldn't hear me either because he, too, was screaming, "Oh my God!"

Our neighbors have a shed in their backyard. For some reason, Alex tried to run through it. But the door wasn't open and he hit it full force. I was maybe twenty feet behind him and closing, so when he hit the door, he kind of bounced back into my arms. I pulled him to the ground. He lay facedown with his back still on fire. I used my arms to put out the flames.

Hannah had been watching us from the house. After the bottle exploded, she yelled to Dan, "I think Alex is on fire." Dan ran toward us and I screamed, "Call nine-one-one!" Dan turned back toward the house and—somehow—Alex got up and followed, with me in tow. I could see strips of charred black skin hanging off his right arm, and patches of red-and-white skin. White skin indicates third-degree burns. We couldn't see his chest because his shirt never caught on fire, but the skin underneath did.

We lived about ten minutes from the closest emergency room, in New Prague, Minnesota. Instead of waiting for the ambulance, Dan drove about ninety miles an hour, and we got there in five minutes. We stormed into the emergency room. The nurses took one look at Alex, cut off his shirt, and immediately covered him in gauze soaked in saline, to bring down the temperature. We didn't know that you need to put cold or ice water on a burn immediately, otherwise the burning continues. But that's all they could do. An ambulance took Alex to Hennepin County Medical Center (HCMC) in Minneapolis, where he was admitted. The doctor said Alex had been burned on over 25 percent of his body and he could expect to stay in the hospital for at least three weeks, maybe more.

ALEX: I was fifteen and about to start my sophomore year in high school. I ran track: the 100 meters, and the four-by-one and four-by-two relays. I played running back on the football team. And now half of my right hand, the inside of my forearm, my armpit, my right biceps, shoulder, and pec, and a little bit of my back were covered in third-degree burns. I had second-degree burns on the right side of my neck and on my right ear.

In the movies, when someone is about to die or is going through an incredibly dangerous situation, we sometimes see their lives flash before them. That actually happened to me while I was on fire and running. I saw my girlfriend, my family, my dogs, and all sorts of happy memories. Then I blacked out and came to lying on the ground by the shed, my mom on top of me. I blacked out again, but remember getting to New Prague. I woke up again in the ambulance on the way to Minneapolis. The EMT asked what my pain level was and I said zero because of how much medication I'd already been given. The worst part was waking up in the scrub room at HCMC. I was lying on a big cart with a plastic mat under me, and nurses were cutting off dead skin with scissors and using some kind of rough sponge and antibiotic solution to debride me. I stayed awake long enough to realize that the pain was unbearable. Then I passed out.

DAN: The family agreed that we would not assign blame. No one could say, "You should've done this or that." The accident was no one's fault. Instead we thought of it as a huge bump in the road, and that we would all be okay. We are all very strongly faith based. Our church formed prayer chains. We stayed positive.

And why not? Alex didn't die. We were together. Our immediate job was to figure out how to work together as a family. Too often, we tend to focus on the bad things in life, but it's much easier on us if we try to find the blessings in every situation.

ALEX: I didn't want to pity myself. I wanted to focus on getting better. I knew that I could. I knew that I would. I thought of what had happened as simply another sports injury. I've been in sports since I was four, and been knocked around plenty. I've had concussions. I got hit in the nose with a baseball. I wanted to work through this new challenge and get back out into the real world. I wanted to play sports and do better in school. I had to fight the fire with that desire.

DAN: Alex had an incredible will to not only beat this but play football as soon as he could. I had no doubt that he would. Alex has to be the strongest person I've ever known. Less than forty-eight hours after the accident, he was already up and walking the halls—slowly—and trying to get stronger before surgery to harvest skin from the back of his thighs for the third-degree burns on his right arm, right hand, and a small portion of his chest and maybe his back. Alex actually considered himself lucky. His neighbor at HCMC was scheduled to have skin harvested and placed on his burned face. Alex thanked God that he didn't have to go through that.

SUZY: Thank God Alex's face was preserved. When I pictured how his arm and chest looked, I couldn't bear to imagine what his life would have been like if his face had been burned. And it could have been. As the ambulance got ready to go to HCMC, Alex's dear sweet girlfriend, Hannah, kissed him good-bye on the lips, then turned to me and said, "All I taste is gas!" Alex had gas on his face, but it never caught on fire, which is amazing. His favorite nurse said, "Alex must have had an angel on his shoulder that night to protect his beautiful face." That got me through the worst of it.

ALEX: I cried once in the hospital from the pain, but otherwise I was happy that I'd been the one to burn. I couldn't have handled it to see my mom on fire.

SUZY: No matter how determined Alex was to get better quickly, the trauma he experienced can play terrible mind games with anyone, not to mention a kid. Alex appeared to be dealing with it, at least on the surface, but we brought in a psychologist anyway. I stayed in his hospital room every night, and once, at 3:00 a.m. Alex started kicking his feet and swinging his good arm. I rubbed his arm to wake him from the dream. He opened his eyes and punched me hard in the chest. He mumbled an apology and said someone had been chasing him. I think it was the fire.

The nurses came in constantly, any time of day or night, so we were often up late watching television. We couldn't believe—and had never noticed before—how many people on fire you see on television. And very little of it is at all realistic, like in the movie *Nacho Libre*. Jack Black catches on fire and runs out of a church for a hundred yards or so. Then he drops, rolls around, stands up, and there's not a burn mark on him.

DAN: Eight days after the accident, the doctors removed Alex's bandages for the first time to evaluate the grafts and remaining burns. We were scared, yet hopeful that the grafts had taken and that the remaining wounds would heal on their own. If so, the surgeries would be over and rehabilitation could begin— all of which would bring us closer to the day we could take Alex home.

SUZY: An amazing thing happened when I asked God to help Alex. One Saturday evening around 11:00 p.m., the nurses asked me to leave the room because they needed to change Alex's bandages. Not only can removing the bandages be painful, but the nurses have to scrub off any blisters that have formed. I retired to the guest area and sat in a corner. I asked God to give Alex strength to get through this. I asked God to help the nurses to be gentle. Most important, I asked for God to just be in that room at that moment to watch over Alex. While I was praying, a vision popped into my head of Jesus standing in Alex's room behind the nurses as they worked on him. Jesus had on a white robe and held both hands up in the air over Alex. I tried to fix that vision in my mind as I continued to pray, because it brought me peace to see Jesus in Alex's room, pouring out His healing on him. Finally, I asked God for some type of sign so that I would know that He was hearing my prayers.

The next day, Sunday, my husband, Dan, brought me the *Star Tribune* Sunday paper. I randomly opened to page B1, and there was a large picture of Jesus in that white robe, with his hands held up, just like in my vision. That proved to me that Jesus is watching over those who face tragedies and hears our prayers.

ALEX: My biggest challenge was going from being a very athletic kid, jumping around, playing football, to not being able to get out of bed. I needed a lot of help just with that. The physical therapists would come in and say, "All right, time to get up." I'd always groan and say, "I don't want to." One person had to grab one side and help me up, and my dad would take my burned arm to cradle it. Standing up was the most painful thing, but when they told me that every day I spent in bed was one more week in the hospital, that motivated me.

SUZY: The doctor told us that Alex would be in the hospital for at least three weeks. He left after only thirteen days. I was amazed, but given what I know about Alex's commitment to himself, not surprised. And he kept a great sense of humor throughout the ordeal. The nurses loved that he never complained and was always happy and joking around. One of the evening nurses was an ex-football player and came in to talk football with Alex every night.

ALEX: When I was in the hospital, I had to sleep with my right arm out. I couldn't move it or the scars would tighten and my arm would curl in and be stuck to my side. The day before I left the hospital, the staff made a splint to keep my arm up all the time. It was incredibly uncomfortable. We ended up using pillows instead. The first night at home I couldn't even sleep in my own little bed, so my dad did and I slept in the California King bed with my mom.

DAN: Because Alex had to sleep with his arm out, Suzy had to curl up toward the bottom part of the bed so she wouldn't run into his arm. It was a very challenging situation for both of them.

Even more challenging was what we went through to change his bandages. We needed Jesus to watch over us as much as we'd needed Him to watch over the nurses. To call it torturous is an understatement. At first we needed two and a half hours. We used blunt-nose scissors to slowly take off the bandages without sticking, but with open wounds, something is always going to stick—and that was hard. Alex stood in the shower, and I installed a handheld showerhead so we could drizzle water on the bandage and work it off. Then we'd drizzle water over the wounds as lightly as we could, and use antibiotic soap to gently work the wounds. Alex was as patient as he could be.

The open wounds look like something you'd get from a bike crash. They're puss-y- and oozy-looking because your body keeps working to get the contaminants out. After Alex air-dried, we had to wrap him up again using an antibacterial mesh called

Adaptec and a mixture of three different cream antibiotics called Bactroban. We mushed the cream into the Adaptec mesh and then placed the mesh over the open wound. Then we wrapped him with gauze and Ace wraps.

SUZY: Once a week we had to go to the burn center for the nurses to remove the bandages so the doctors could check the grafts. Some sections naturally bubble up and almost look like brain matter, but they had to burn them off with silver nitrate, after a topical numbing cream is applied. Sometimes Alex could still feel the burn, and once we had a nurse who was extremely rough. She ripped off the bandages in a way that made a six-foot-tall kid cry, and then put silver nitrate on areas she hadn't numbed. We're normally very patient and courteous, but I completely lost it and yelled at the nurse supervisor. We even made an arrangement to go in an hour early the next time so that Dan and I could be the ones to take off the bandages before the doctor arrived.

ALEX: Having to work so hard just to get out of bed affected other parts of my life. I promised myself to reapply myself and do better at school, and I became a better person. I wouldn't wish what I went through on anyone, but I like the way I am now and would choose to do it this way again.

My friends are of course curious. They want to know how bad it hurt. I tell them it was like nothing they've ever experienced. Some ask if they can see and touch my burns. I don't mind at all. I could have worn my compression shirt another year if I'd wanted to, just to make the scars look better, but I didn't care. I like the way they look now. But I have to be careful. Grafted skin doesn't have sweat or oil glands. I'm always putting on lotion, and when it gets hot, in the summer or during workouts, I have to stay conscious of overheating.

Even after my wounds healed, I'd hold my arms close to my-self, like I was lame. During the football season, I was supposed to be on the field with the varsity team, but I got nervous that the players would hit my arm, so I stayed in the stands.

DAN: But we all got through. Our primary source of inspiration was the family's faith in God and knowing His ability to heal, plus the love we felt for each other. The other part was CaringBridge.

Suzy and I were using e-mail to communicate about Alex until one of Suzy's friends said, "You should start a CaringBridge site." Suzy mentioned it to me and I said, "I don't think so. We're only going to be in the burn ward for a couple weeks." I thought CaringBridge was about people with cancer who were terminally ill or were in a very long and devastating situation. My perception was that Alex didn't qualify for the site. I was wrong, and when we read the encouraging words from people who signed the guest book, that was huge. Kids from school would voice their support. Kids on the football teams wrote to say that they missed him. He got tons of birthday wishes when he turned sixteen.

He got inspirational messages like this:

> *"Behind every success is effort...*
> *Behind every effort is passion...*
> *Behind every passion is someone with the courage to try."*
> —unknown
>
> *"It's not the mountains we conquer, but ourselves."*
> —Sir Edmund Hillary
>
> *You are an inspiration to others. God bless!*

We read the guest book to Alex every night.

ALEX: I've been asked more than once why I never posted to

170

the journal. Simple, actually. I really only had one good hand, and I usually had two or three IVs in that arm. I could barely even lift it at times.

SUZY: CaringBridge helped us get the word out about Alex to our family who didn't live near. Also, Alex is involved in a Christian youth group called Young Life, a faith-based organization for teens. The summer before his accident he had gone on a Young Life retreat to Colorado and met people from all over the United States. When Alex's Young Life leader heard what happened, he read our CaringBridge journal and posted it out to all the Young Life leaders, who then told all their kids. We had thousands of people praying for Alex because we had communicated through CaringBridge.

ALEX: The summer before the accident, I had a bad attitude about everything and didn't really care about anything. I fought with my parents a lot, and nothing was going that well for me. Now we have a great relationship. It's been nice. My mom and my dad were there for me every day in the hospital, and I know it. You don't really notice how much your parents love you until something really tragic happens. Life is short and you never know when it's going to end. Don't waste it.

SUZY: If there's one message we'd like readers to take away from Alex's story, it's to *never* use gas on a fire. We learned that the hardest way imaginable.

DAN: Bad things can happen, but with your faith, your family, and your friends you can overcome anything. I believe with all my heart that those three components kept us strong as a family and allowed Alex to have the great attitude that he has. We have no doubt that he'll use this story to help other kids, and other people. Weird things happen and a lot of times we don't know why, but we know that Alex's story will make life better for someone else.

How to Start a Prayer Chain

Praying is one of the most ancient of human practices, and to this day billions of people still believe in its power. Prayer transcends religions, denominations, sects, and belief systems of all kinds. It's used in a multitude of ways: to seek comfort, make a request, ask for guidance, heal and restore, express sorrow, celebrate joy, give thanks. At its most elemental level, with everything else stripped away, praying is simply talking to someone (importantly, someone who's always happy to listen).

A *prayer chain* kicks it up several levels, because it is a group of individuals who've decided to pray together. This theoretically amplifies the power of prayer.

Praying as a group also fulfills another of our basic human needs: to connect, both with a power greater than ourselves and with one another.

Here are some guidelines that will help you and others in your sphere have an effective prayer chain—one that's ready to pray for any person or any cause at any time.

- *Decide whom to include in your prayer chain.* They should be dependable and willing to join in prayer at a moment's notice. These individuals can also expand the chain even more with like-minded people they know. Think about including your faith community, family, friends, neighbors, and colleagues.
- *Communicating prayer requests.* You used to be limited to phone calls and word of mouth. Now you can post re-

quests on someone's CaringBridge site or other social networks, or build an e-mail list that allows you to send prayer requests to everyone with one click.

- *Prayer requests may not always come with an explanation.* The patient may prefer privacy. A request can just be a top-line explanation, such as "Please pray for a woman who's moving into long-term care on Monday."
- *Share information right away.* If you get word that the situation of one of your prayer recipients has changed, communicate it to everyone in your prayer chain so they can adjust their prayers.

MEGHANN AND DEREK DEROSIER

Caleb the Incredible

Dr. Meghann Derosier is a recently minted family physician, thanks to a Health Professional Scholarship from the US Air Force, for which she owes three years' service. Stationed at Andrews Air Force Base, she was deployed to Afghanistan for her first assignment. Sgt. Derek Derosier served in the US Army for four years, and spent fourteen months in Iraq. When their daughter, Abbie, was born, Derek became a part-time stay-at-home dad ("A SAHD," he says), and when their son, Caleb, arrived, Derek graduated to full-time SAHD.

Caleb was seven months old when Meghann and Derek noticed that Caleb's testicles were swollen. "He didn't seem to mind," Meghann remembers. "He was a happy baby, always laughing, smiling, in good spirits. But in just a couple of days the swelling increased and began to bother him."

The Derosiers, then living in Bangor, Maine, took him to the doctor. After an ultrasound, he was diagnosed with an infection and prescribed antibiotics. "But he kept getting worse," says Meghann. "He wasn't sleeping. He began throwing up."

Caleb's parents rushed him to the hospital. After drawing

blood, the hospital sent the family back to their two-bedroom townhouse to await the results.

"We were putting the kids to bed—Abbie was almost two and had her own room; Caleb slept in a crib in our bedroom—when the phone rang," says Derek, who walked into the living room just as Meghann hung up.

"We have to go to the hospital," she said, turning to her husband, ashen-faced. "Caleb has leukemia."

MEGHANN: We called Derek's sister-in-law, Katy, to ask if she could watch Abbie. She came right over and said out loud what we'd been thinking: "It just can't be true." To hear the word *leukemia* was unreal. The words *child* and *cancer* should never be part of the same sentence.

At the hospital they told us that Caleb's white cell count was 857,000. Normal for little kids is 5,000 to 10,000. Being a doctor, that scared me more than anything. I realized that he could have a stroke before they were even able to start treating his leukemia. The oncologist didn't sugarcoat it at all. Caleb had acute myeloid leukemia (AML), type M4. His myeloid cells—immature white blood cells—were the problem. This cancer is present in only 3 percent of the average population. It was so aggressive that it infiltrated everywhere in Caleb: under his skin, in his spinal fluid, in his brain. No part of his body was untouched. His white blood cells *were* the cancer cells.

She did not expect him to make it.

At that moment our lives changed in a way that every parent fears: the possibility that we could lose someone we loved so much. We couldn't imagine how we'd even breathe if the unthinkable happened.

In a way I was angry with myself. I'm a doctor, and yet when I saw the swollen testicles, leukemia was not even on my list of differential diagnoses. During the week, even though Caleb got sicker, he was on antibiotics—so it was easy for me to say, "Well, he's throwing up because of the antibiotics." I'm not sure how I justified his not sleeping, but I could justify everything else. It all hit me at the hospital when the doctor said, "Wow, he looks pale. His belly looks big," as soon as he walked into the room. I hadn't seen that. I had been in mom mode.

We asked our oncologist, "Was that swollen testicle cancer?"

"We'll never know," she said. "It could just have been an infection, but the last little thing Caleb's body needed before it pushed over to cancer." It took a while for me not to feel guilty, but eventually I realized that had Caleb been someone else's child brought to my office, I wouldn't necessarily have seen the leukemia either. This is actually a very common story with kids and leukemia. Doctors will treat for an ear infection or pneumonia three times before finding out it's something else. In hindsight any doctor would wish they'd caught the disease earlier, but when you're in the exam room, you think that you're doing everything right.

DEREK: Caleb's illness was beyond stressful. At first, I overwhelmed Meghann with medical questions when it was more important to let her be a mother trying to love and care for her son. But during Caleb's full-body MRI, I was in the room with our son while Meghann was behind the glass, looking over the technician's shoulder, at the computer. What she saw made her break down. The nurse rushed in and insisted that I come with her. I found Meghann staring at all the white spots on the screen, saying, "That's not normal. That's not normal." She thought the worst, and it wasn't until after the MRI that what she thought were cancer cells turned out to be nothing to worry about. They say that knowledge is power, but sometimes it's not always helpful.

Caleb continued to get sores on his back that looked like something out of a horror movie. The doctors weren't sure if they were bacterial or viral, so they loaded him up with heavy-duty antibiotics and antifungal meds, and those drugs made it harder to control issues that the chemo and leukemia were already messing with. And to top it off, Caleb was teething. We couldn't get a break. It was harder and harder to change his diaper because of the pain. Just touching Caleb's legs made him cry as if we were twisting them off. His belly was swollen again.

All Meghann and I could do was pray and be grateful for all the prayers coming from around the world. We cried for Caleb, but we were given strength knowing that he was touching the lives of so many.

As emotional as it was then, and as emotional as it often got, I had to stay strong for our family. I had to be even-keeled, level-headed, not lose my cool. It's the same battlefield condition as when I was in Iraq as a forward observer. You can't overreact or become emotional; you have to focus on what you need to do and where you need to go. Take care of the people you can take care of, and yourself, and not sweat the small stuff. With Caleb I didn't get that right away, but now I see that being in the military made me stronger and more mentally stable. Meghann and I turned to each other and to God for inspiration and strength. Our faith deepened. We've always been religious, but I never prayed so hard.

MEGHANN: That first night the doctors put a central line in Caleb and he had a blood exchange. That means using one big syringe to take out bad blood full of immature white blood cells, and put in good donated blood with a syringe through another port. The next day Caleb started chemotherapy via a spinal tap. He was only seven months old and weighed twenty-two pounds.

Thank goodness he had no idea what was going on. Derek and I on the other hand kept trying to wrap our heads around the big turn our lives had taken. We tried not to let ourselves cry around Caleb, but that didn't work some of the time.

When Caleb went into the hospital, he was the sickest person in the ICU. For two weeks his condition was touch and go. Every Friday, the ICU doctors would have a family meeting with us and ask disturbing questions: "What is too much for you?" "When do you want us to withdraw care?" That kept it real, but we said, "There is no point where we would want to stop care." Probably there would be a point, if necessary, but when we saw Caleb, even though he was very uncomfortable and couldn't move without pain, we knew he was still in there.

DEREK: Abbie stayed with my brother and sister-in-law for a week before she came to see Caleb. We told her that Caleb's blood was sick. The first time she visited, she stood up on the crib and gave him a big kiss on the head, which is where she always kisses him. He smiled for the first time. After that, the only time he would smile was when Abbie visited.

MEGHANN: After two weeks, Caleb had his first bone marrow biopsy to see how he did with his first round of chemo. Was he in partial remission, complete remission, or did he still have more than 5 percent leukemia? That decides whether you're high- or low-risk, and sometimes whether or not you're likely to live.

After one round of chemo, Caleb went from having all that cancer in him to having zero percent cancer. What a relief. Caleb had a long road still ahead, of chemo, a bone marrow transplant, constant monitoring, emergencies, and last-minute recoveries, but he's stayed in remission ever since. In our CaringBridge journal we had begun calling Caleb "Caleb the Incredible," just because he'd been so brave. With the good news, he became even more incredible.

Even though Caleb was ill, Meghann had to start her air force service. She had been assigned to Luke Air Force Base in Arizona. Derek and Meghann had already been there, found a beautiful home with a pool, and started paying rent. They had a rubber stamp made with their new return address. They had tickets to take Abbie to shows. And then their normal life ground to a halt, as, says Derek, "a wrench was thrown into the gears." Meghann petitioned the air force to change her assignment. She wanted Hanscom AFB in Massachusetts, but they were overstaffed. Lackland AFB in San Antonio was another alternative. In the interim, the family went to Andrews AFB outside of Washington, DC, to await the final decision. That meant Caleb could continue his treatment in good hands at Walter Reed, where the family was thrilled to learn that the doctors believed that Caleb should do five rounds of chemo instead of get a bone marrow transplant. While in temporary housing, Meghann and Derek hoped to locate near Bethesda, Maryland, but the air force decided Andrews would work for everyone.

MEGHANN: From the very beginning, CaringBridge was part of our lives. But we decided not to write in it as Meghann and Derek, but in Caleb's voice. We wanted to keep the details of Caleb's journey in perspective and add a little comic relief at a time that was filled with so many difficulties and despair. An adult voice could easily get hung up there, but a child's perspective would be more innocent and pure, even as "he" conveyed adult information in a way that we hoped was delightful, funny, spry, matter-of-fact, brave, and wise. Drawing on how he inspired us, and what we observed by being with him all the time, we created and extrapolated Caleb's personality for the world. Another reason we wrote the journal from Caleb's perspective is so readers wouldn't say, "Oh, Meghann wrote this," or "Did you read what Derek wrote?" We liked the invisibility. It made us more secure and willing to share.

Hello all!

Today was a pain in my bee-hind!! Literally! My bum has taken a beating from all this chemo pee and poo and has a horrible rash on it. Mama and Papa have been putting "butt paste" on it and changing me like it's no one's business, but I have still managed to get one heck of a sore bottom. The docs are worried about it getting infected, so tonight I have been prescribed some antibacterial ointment to help battle any bacteria that have set up camp there. Mama went and got me a big tub of maximum-strength Desitin to see if that will do the trick too. We are trying everything!!

My body still has a few white blood cells living and they are a little elevated today, as they are probably trying to heal my very sore backside. So with any luck, I will be able to get this diaper rash under control before all my healing cells die off because of the chemo . . . it could be a long three weeks! So, heal, diaper rash, heal!

I enjoyed my afternoon because I got to have my first audition for the Full Monty. Yep, no diaper for me! Mama and Papa were letting me "air out" down there and were good sports about the tinkling I did. Only one pee got out of hand. It really was easier this way anyway because so many docs wanted to see my backside, and it was right there out in the open for all to see—and admire, might I add. HEHE!

Today, Gabe the chemo duck was given to Mama and Papa for Abbie to have. He is a duck that has a bandanna on his head (with a matching one for Abbie) and has a Hickman catheter on his chest just like me! This way when Abbie gets here, she can have Gabe to learn about what I have on my body and pretend to be a doctor too! She can even give Gabe medicine when I get my medicine. She will learn in no time how to take care of me and, I am sure, be one of the reasons I will get better so quickly!! I am excited to have her by my side again.

Well, Papa is cuddling with me tonight; I have taken a liking to sleeping with one of them close by. I am not a fan of my crib anymore. I like it much better in the big-boy bed with one of them. It makes me feel safe and secure, so I can focus on getting some good sleep to help me heal and recover.

Well, it's off to dreamland for me. Sweet dreams, everyone.

Love, Caleb

DEREK: We not only shared with the readers, but the journal helped Meghann and me share with each other. I had kept a journal when I was in Iraq, knowing that someday Meghann would read it. I told her in the journal what I couldn't tell her on the phone. I filled two journals and gave them to her when I got back. The journals became an emotional pathway for me to communicate with my wife.

MEGHANN: Using the online journal let Derek and I communicate in real time, especially after we got stationed at Andrews Air Force Base and Caleb was admitted to Walter Reed hospital to start his second round of chemo and complete his treatments. We set up a routine where one of us would be at the hospital for a day and a half, then we'd meet and switch places. When we were on duty, we did our update at night, which let the parent at home know what had happened when they were away. And since we had a huge collection of people who followed Caleb the Incredible's progress, we didn't have so many calling to ask how he was.

But for Derek and me, the journal was more than what you saw on the surface. You had to read between the lines. We were able to get to know the person we'd decided to spend our lives with, and watch as they were vigilant, an awesome caretaker, and deeply connected to our sick child. It made my heart grow. We could thank each other by mentioning, in Caleb's voice, how strong Mama and Papa were. I did that often, and he did, too. We were able to stay close as a couple—which many parents have a tough time with when they're on opposite schedules and totally consumed with a sick child. What seems strange now, and maybe a bit naive, is that I don't think we ever truly fathomed that what we wrote would be e-mailed and forwarded and shared with so many others. But that additional benefit definitely helped me stay stronger, because we had so many prayers and so much support from people we didn't even know.

DEREK: Once in a great while we'd write in our own voice. I remember wanting Caleb to have someone that he could one day look back on to have an idea about what his mother and father were going through.

Dear Caleb,

In the course of one week, our world has been shaken, turned around, and thrown in every direction, and still you are the amazing boy that filled our hearts and home with laughter, smiles, and love. I sit here with you this evening alone, and I feel helpless, weak, and scared. I wish more than anything in the world I could take this from you. I wish I knew what to do to fix the pain you are in. I wish you would tell me everything is going to be okay. I look to you for strength and think you are more of a man at seven months than I'll ever be.

Your mother and I are overjoyed with the outpouring of love and support, and know that there is a higher reason for all of this. We know with all the prayers that have been sent your way, God, the Angels, and the Saints are all watching over you, and you will make it through this, you are not alone. You are strong, a fighter and everyone can see this in your eyes and your smile. All I ask is that you keep fighting, and then fight some more. I need you, Caleb.

I look at you and I admire the strength you have and I try to think of the man you will grow into. Each day you amaze me and show me what it means to have faith and love. One day, you will again fill our home with laughter, smiles, and love, and I can't wait.

MEGHANN: It was Caleb's first birthday. He had finally been discharged from Walter Reed earlier in the month. That night I also wrote a letter to Caleb. I shared with my son—and Derek—feelings that, at the time, I just didn't have the emotional capacity to say out loud.

January 30

Happy Birthday to my amazing son.

Today has been such a great day, and it was all because we were celebrating you. You have triumphed and are truly incredible. We have been beside you and watching in awe at your amazement each and every day.

I think back to a year ago and how blessed we felt to have you in our lives from the very first second. You are a blessing from God! Now here we are…almost one month at our new home and you are on the go. Your crawling is now officially a crawl, and no sooner have you mastered that than you are on to trying to stand and cruise around. You will be walking in no time. You are strong beyond your year(s).

When I look at you, I see a little boy who will never know the battles he's won, just as I will never know how you summoned such bravery at times of our greatest despair. You have helped us rise up when we had fallen. We found our greatest strength from God because of the will you fought with and how you persevered. Not only did you heal yourself, but you also helped heal your family's questioning and heartache.

You have taught me so much, Caleb. I am stronger than I ever knew I was and have found a newfound appreciation for every second of every day. Seeing you smile and laugh or have Abbie give you an unexpected kiss makes my heart full and my life content. But most importantly, I have truly learned that God is always with us and protecting us before we ever begin to ask for help.

Life is good…my children are healthy and my family is together. We now live in the today instead of waiting for a better tomorrow. Because of you, a day of playing in the house is as good as Disneyland. My priorities are forever changed.

I trust that God is on our side and, as so many have told us, you are healed and over this battle. I will always pray that you never have to deal with such a battle for health again.

Happy First Birthday to a little boy who has shown so many others the true meaning of life, and made his mother so proud.

Caleb, you are incredible and I love you beyond words!

Mama

The next day Caleb posted that I had hogged the computer, and said that he had pretended to be sleepy so I wouldn't feel guilty.

When the time comes, Caleb is definitely more than welcome to look at everything. We're saving it for him. He is better now, still in remission after two years, and he will never remember any of what happened. But he will have scars on his body, and I guess one day he'll ask about them and that's where we'll start.

This journey has changed me in many ways. It has strengthened our marriage and made us both appreciate the kids more. I've also changed as a doctor. Because of Caleb, I'm committed to humanizing medicine. I want patients to understand what's going on. I like to show patients their labs so they know exactly what the numbers are and mean instead of just saying, "Everything looks good." This experience has made me much more aware of how the doctor-patient relationship can be more than just what the doctor does during an appointment. People should know what they can do and how they can be their own advocate.

The biggest lesson I learned from Caleb's getting sick is that you can't keep planning. That's the takeaway. You have to live in the day, live in the moment, cherish each moment as it comes. Now, before I go to Afghanistan, faced with having to leave Caleb, Abbie, and Derek for so long, I know that I'm going to miss so many of those little moments again. But then I try to look at it from a challenge perspective and from a religious aspect. I know that this is God's mountain for me right now. I would much rather have this mountain in front of me than Caleb relapsing. I would much rather miss eight months of being with my family if it means that Caleb, Abbie, and Derek will all be safe and healthy—and there when I return.

Hi friends and family!

Today marks the second anniversary of being diagnosed with AML and nineteen months posttreatment. Mama and Papa remember all too well the phone call that changed our family forever. But in spite of the terrible news that evening, good has prevailed. Thanks to the great treatment at both Eastern Maine Medical Center and Walter Reed, I am now a normal two-year-old. Well, two and a half, but who's counting?

With love,
Caleb the Incredible

"When we honestly ask ourselves which person in our lives means the most to us, we often find that it is those who, instead of giving advice, solutions, or cures, have chosen rather to share our pain and touch our wounds with a warm and tender hand. The friend who can be silent with us in a moment of despair or confusion, who can stay with us in an hour of grief and bereavement, who can tolerate not knowing, not curing, not healing and face with us the reality of our powerlessness, that is a friend who cares."

—*Henri J. M. Nouwen*, The Road to Daybreak: A Spiritual Journey

LAUREN LICHTEL

The Bad-Luck Train

My husband, Marty, and I had been together for about seven years when, as the summer approached, we decided to try to get pregnant. We got lucky in October and found out in early November. Breaking the news to our families at Thanksgiving dinner seemed like great timing.

Just before the holiday I was lying in bed, watching TV, and idly touching my left breast. It felt tender and sore, as breasts tend to feel during pregnancy, but then I found a lump. I'd done self-exams for years, so I was immediately concerned. And yet I knew that pregnancy tended to change a woman's breasts, and I was still at the early stages. I asked Marty what he thought, and he said, "Oh, it's probably nothing."

Our families were overjoyed at the baby news. I didn't mention anything about my breast. But I was still sore, and the lump remained. The week after Thanksgiving I had a scheduled ultrasound and exam and I asked the doctor to investigate. "I think it's probably just a clogged milk duct," I said. She palpated the area and said, "That's *not* a clogged milk duct. You need to get that biopsied. Now."

At the Comprehensive Breast Health Center of Brigham and Women's Hospital, I underwent a biopsy and an ultrasound of the breast tissue and lymph nodes. It hurt like hell. Afterward, dressing in the exam room, I felt like I was in the wrong place, the Twilight Zone, and that I didn't belong there. From the studied impassivity of the tech's face I was sure that something wasn't right. She didn't say anything—they aren't allowed to—and I didn't ask. But I knew. I had a gut feeling. It was cancer. *It was cancer.* But all the doctor said was, "We can't tell you *for sure* what it is right now." *It's cancer.* "We have to send it out." *It's cancer. I know it.* Because I was very young and also pregnant, she promised to get the results sooner than the usual five to seven days.

That night at home I couldn't contain myself. "It's cancer," I told Marty. "It's cancer. It's got to be cancer." Marty tried to calm me, but I was driven, as if repeating my worst fear over and over, would keep it from coming true.

Two days later, while my dad and I sat on the couch at my house, the phone rang.

"Is this Lauren Lichtel?"

"Yes."

"This is the doctor's office. You have breast cancer. We need to see you at four o'clock today." And that was that. No lead-in. No comforting words. No soft landing. Just, "You have breast cancer." It's not okay to shatter someone's life over the phone and then tell them to wait three hours before they can come in. My reaction was R rated.

I hung up, shaking, cursing, crying. I had to force myself not to hyperventilate and to be strong for my dad, because he had already dealt with too much cancer in his life: his mom, his wife, himself. And now me.

I called Marty and he said he'd rush home. My dad left to pick up my mom. For ten minutes I was alone and half-paralyzed. I called a nearby friend who was also pregnant. She came over and found me in the bathroom, staring at myself in the mirror, crying and sobbing and repeating to myself, "You have to stop. You have to stop. It's not good for the baby. You can't do this." She wrapped a blanket around me and held me so tightly that I literally had to stop shaking.

Then I let loose. "Fuck! I'm twenty-six! Who in their right mind at twenty-six thinks about cancer?" I knew kids got cancer—a horrible thought—but otherwise I believed that it waited until you were older. In your twenties you're supposed to think about getting married, buying a house, a career, kids. Not breast-effing-cancer.

Was I feeling sorry for myself? Yes. Was I behaving poorly? What's the proper reaction to a terrible diagnosis? Should I have just kept a positive attitude, and "battled" my cancer like the support groups advise? Perhaps. But not then.

During the days that followed I couldn't sleep. I vomited a lot. I had weird dreams. I peed so often that I thought my bladder would explode. At night I'd be in and out of bed, kept awake by my fear and my nausea. When I tried to snuggle with Marty, I only made him wake up long before he had to. I was a human alarm clock that kept going off early.

Sometimes I wondered how my dad handled all that cancer years ago, his mom and wife sick at the same time, having to go back and forth, not to mention his own cancer. Perhaps it's a generational thing, stoicism: "Yeah, okay. It is what it is. We'll try to fix it. Whatever. Don't upset the world while you're at it."

For me it was like a death sentence. *There's no cure. There's no definitive, "Yep, you don't have cancer anymore." Even if you're in remission, you have cancer forever.*

I went for a second opinion at Dana-Farber, and the diagnosis was the same. I needed a mastectomy. But there were complications. I was pregnant and couldn't have surgery until the second trimester because the anesthesia is not safe for the baby during the first trimester. I needed chemotherapy, but had to wait until the late second or early third trimesters. If I needed radiation, the baby would be induced around the thirty-seventh week.

Twenty-six years old. Pregnant. Breast cancer. I was on the Bad-Luck Train.

I started my CaringBridge site even before my surgery. I'd heard that writing in the journal would be therapeutic, but for me it was simply a way to share information, because everybody and their brother wanted a piece of me. "Give me a call." "What's going on?" "Let's meet for coffee." I know they meant well, but I'd cry hysterically just talking to my grandmother.

Every day I'd relive the bad-news phone call. I asked my mom, "How long until cancer isn't the first thing on your brain when you wake up in the morning and the last thing on your brain when you go to bed at night?"

"It takes a long time," she said. "But you'll get there."

At least with CaringBridge I could just say, "Hey, go to this website. I need my space."

That's what I intended, but from the outset my journal became the place I could transcend mere information and vent. I shared whatever came into my head, stream of consciousness, and I didn't care who read it. Instead of worrying what everyone thought, like when I'd sucked in my stomach during high school so I wouldn't look as fat as I thought I looked, I let it all hang out and then some. On Christmas Eve I wrote, "Isn't this supposed to be a joyous occasion?! We are supposed to be surrounded by family and celebrating this wonderful holiday. All I feel like doing is crying myself to sleep. And then I will wake up four hours later to empty my exploding bladder. Are you allowed to swear on here?"

"How are you doing?" seemed to be the most popular question. I didn't know, and I couldn't lie just to reassure everyone. I couldn't put on a brave face and dress myself in positive thinking. My answer: "I don't know how to answer that."

Many friends offered to introduce me to other breast cancer patients or survivors for guidance. I appreciated the support, but I had to be honest and hope no one took my answer personally. "No." I wasn't ready. I worried about everything from my unborn baby to how I'd look in a bathing suit next summer. Would my treatment hurt my baby? Or would I have to wait so long it would hurt me? Would I have one good boob and one nonboob, a perky one and a saggy one? Would everyone look at me funny? Would I have to walk around in ninety-degree summer heat in a huge sweatshirt to hide my hideous, deformed body?

Then I saw a news story about Santa visiting the Children's Hospital so that kids who couldn't go outside would know that Santa could still find them, and I realized it wasn't all about me. When I saw an eight-year-old girl with leukemia, I burst into tears. There I was stressing out about my cancer—legitimately— but what must someone so innocent and so sick be going through? If she could fight, so could I—and I'd be fighting for two. Then it struck me that if my baby was born on or around its due date, its astrological sign would be Cancer.

So many of those early days were filled with questions: Why am I going through all of this?! Why don't some people understand what it's like? And anger: that I had to wait for surgery while I felt the lump in my breast grow and worried it would spread to my lymph nodes; that I had to have chemotherapy during my pregnancy; that I wouldn't get my fake boob until after the baby was born; that I'd start each day crying or puking or both; angry that every reasonable delay and the million questions I got asked at each doctor's appointment felt like a major inconvenience. Anger that my life had run off the rails. Anger at all the anger.

The reality that I would lose my hair hit me while shampooing it in the shower. I spent ten minutes just running my fingers through my hair wondering what it would be like to not be able to do that. My long, thick red hair had always been one of my identifying characteristics. I couldn't get that hair color from a bottle! And when it grew back, if it did, would it be the same? Rather than get a wig, I decided I'd cut it beforehand and have a wig made of my *own* hair.

Then one morning Marty rolled over in bed, on my hair—ow!—and I laughed because soon I wouldn't have to worry about that hurting anymore. My sense of humor had become dark and twisted, like Meredith Grey's on *Grey's Anatomy*. It was the only way to cope. But sometimes when I made a joke about not being here or dying, people just stared at me. They didn't get it. They didn't know if it was okay to laugh. Not even my husband.

People read my journal and told me I was courageous to be so open. I didn't feel remotely courageous. A friend who had been afraid to go in for her mammogram called me an inspiration because I'd given her the courage to schedule it. That meant the world to me, even though I felt like an ordinary person just trying to survive. My only happy days were when I began to feel my baby bump, heard the baby's heartbeat, got a new ultrasound picture, and felt the baby inside me. What really bothered me was that I wasn't used to depending on others for support. I wanted to be the helper, the best friend. I wanted to be in control. I hated not being in control.

———

After I met with my surgical team, my hope for the future and my attitude began to improve. I am by nature wary of doctors and believe that every patient should strongly advocate for themselves, but the surgeons seemed to know exactly what to do, and explained it wonderfully to Marty and me. The breast and plastic surgeons would remove my breast and put in a temporary implant. It wouldn't be the same size as the original, and it wouldn't feel real, but it would be better than nothing. An alloderm (skin from a dead person) would help hold the temporary in place. I'd get antibiotics. I would not be able to shower or lift my arm for a while. If everything healed as expected, I'd get chemo six weeks later. I'd also be on Herceptin. At least the high-risk ob/gyn told me my baby looked great and gave me a new ultrasound picture. She even said I'd have a chance to breast-feed.

The night before surgery I told my boob "good-bye" and wrote, "Screw you, cancer!" in my journal. Then I went to sleep because we had to be at the hospital at 5:30 a.m. for a 7:30 a.m. procedure. We didn't make it through the night. At 1:00 a.m. Marty and I bolted up to the sound of running water. A pipe had been improperly installed two weeks earlier, leaked slowly, then burst, spewing water all over the living room floor, damaging the basement ceiling and walls that had just been painted. I wrote in my journal: *FLOOD IN MY HOUSE!!! Surgery day. WHAT THE BLOODY FUCK!!!!!!!!!!!???!?!?!?*

We were still riding on the Bad-Luck Train.

Fortunately, the operation went well. Five days later I returned home to a scene of emergency repairs and construction that faded into the background, if only because I was in so much pain that I wanted to rip off my arm—which I could barely lift. My journal entry: *People say that I have been to hell and back. I beg to differ. I'M STILL IN HELL!* Medication helped the physical pain, but the mental anguish left me in tears every time I saw the huge scar across my chest. I wanted my breast back. I wanted the feeling in my arm back. I wanted my house to be normal.

Marty wanted our lives back. He posted:

As for me, I wanted to take a brief opportunity to thank everyone personally for the first time here, for all of your support. It warms my heart to know that there are already over three thousand visits to this web journal. Every day someone new is pledging support for us, and I am very thankful for each and every one of you as we move forward in our difficult journey. The last six weeks overall have been the worst time of my life to date. Just when I thought things were looking up, something inexplicably inconvenient, rare, unlucky, or tragic was waiting to fill the void left by the last miserable event, in a rapid-fire way I've never experienced before. It has had the effect of neatly ripping up most of the usual feel-good phrases like "things happen in threes" and "everything happens for a reason" and "the

worst is over," turning all of it into useless drivel. Understand-
ably, this is not what I expected as I approach my thirtieth
birthday. I have read most of the book Why Bad Things Happen to Good People *and found it very comforting. I have*
come to firmly believe that we are nothing more than the vic-
tims of unfortunate coincidences and that such is the random
nature of life. I look forward to the only real panacea I know of
that can ameliorate our pain—the passing of time.

If only. My pain receded, but the house wasn't finished with
us. Because of construction, the downstairs toilet was not installed, and only rags plugged the sewer-line hole—which had
backed up. Marty cleaned it. Then someone used a plunger in
another bathroom, and the sewage came out the hole. Marty
cleaned it. I packed and went to my mother's house, leaving my
poor husband to deal with insurance adjusters, with getting me
to doctor's appointments in bad traffic and worse weather, with
listening to me complain about how I hurt all over, and with my
anxiety about the cancer coming back.

We did have good news. A post-op exam and pathology results confirmed that the lump had been 2.4 centimeters and that
my margins were clean. The doctor had taken twenty-two lymph
nodes, but only one had cancer—and it had been cancerous *be-*
fore the diagnosis, which meant that the cancer hadn't spread
during my wait for surgery. We scheduled follow-up appointments, and spoke with excitement about the baby that was due in
six months. My last stop that day was the most emotional: with
the wig maker, I also looked at some hats and scarves.

The next morning Marty and I heard a very loud noise in our
living room/dining room area. We found two huge cracks in the
wall between the rooms. The diagnosis? Our roof was collapsing

under the weight of the snow. We needed a structural engineer immediately. Marty and I broke down and walked around the house speechless and crying. We didn't know what to do. I wrote in my journal, *I guess we are not off the Bad-Luck Train after all.*

The next morning ice fell off the roof, landed on our electric meter, and bent it. Our regular electrician was skiing, and the guys who came charged us an arm and a leg. We had to get it fixed right away so that a short wouldn't set the house afire. I felt the money running through our hands like melting snow in a heat wave. I wrote in my journal, *We're screwed.*

We were, but only for a little while. These things pass. Gradually my pain was easier to manage. An ultrasound showed that the baby was very healthy. I scheduled my first chemo for early March and discussed the drugs they'd use, their effectiveness, and their side effects. I would lose my hair—which was, oddly, more upsetting to me than losing my breast—and speculated when it might grow back. I opted to shave it off before it came out in random clumps.

At my next visit to the ob/gyn I felt a flutter and, at the same time, saw the baby's legs kick on the ultrasound. We found out the sex: a girl. We had the name ready—Megan Ashley Lichtel—and she arrived, to our incalculable joy, in June, after my first four rounds of chemo. Having gone through cancer surgery and treatment in parallel with my pregnancy, I found the C-section was practically a breeze. Marty and I were very happy that Megan was out and doing well. What a relief. One day I'll tell Megan how she saved my life. If I hadn't been pregnant, I might not have found the lump in my left breast in time.

———

In any health crisis the healing goes beyond the physical. I shared a lot in my journal, but not everything. After all was said and done, I didn't go into depth about how unattractive and unfeminine I felt. I didn't go on about how the stress caused Marty's and my relationship to become disconnected in some ways and more connected in others. The physical act of sex has never been the *most* important thing in my life, but the intimacy that goes with it is—and the cancer tore away at it. Our sex life has changed and we've worked—with success—to repair it. This is not unusual. It's me: I don't feel attractive. I don't feel that I'm woman enough for my husband. My body just looks different.

I suffer other residual effects. Some days I have to fight really hard to get out of bed. I'm still afraid the cancer will come back and I'll have to go through this all again, so what's the point—I'm going to die in a couple of years and all this will have been for nothing. Or I could benefit from my grandmother's great genes and live to be one hundred.

There has been an upside to the whole experience. While I don't celebrate cancer, like some do, as a blessing inside of a curse, I do view life more positively now. I'm more extreme in seeing the good everywhere. I take everything in stride and with a deep breath first. My marriage has survived. I have a beautiful daughter. Life feels precious. I know that I have one shot at it, one chance to do it in a way that I will be proud of. When I'm on my deathbed, no matter if it's tomorrow or in seventy-five years, I want only to be proud of myself. I want to know that I did as much as I could of everything I wanted to do. I want to know I was a good person, a good wife, a good mother, a good family member, a good friend.

Recently I did something that I would once have found appalling and unimaginable. I had my other breast removed. It wasn't medically necessary. The cancer doesn't jump from one breast to the other. But one day after the final left implant was finished, I found myself idly touching my right breast and wondering, "Is that a lump? Is that a lump? Is *that* a lump?" *I'm young,* I thought. *Is that something I want to do for the next seventy years?* I've got more important concerns: Is my daughter healthy? Is my house all right? What about our financial picture? How's Marty holding up? I wanted to take a worry that I could control out of the picture.

I feel like I've finally gotten off the bad-luck train and watched it leave the station. Without us.

The Benefits of Journaling

Journaling about your health journey can be enormously beneficial. Whether you use a private journal and a pen, or a computer and a keyboard, journaling can provide stress relief, help you understand how far you've come, and give you an outlet for your emotions. It can also serve as a reminder of how you reacted to procedures and medications. If you decide to keep an online journal, you will give your friends and family a better understanding of your situation and how they can help. Connecting with your circle might result in more than a refrigerator full of casserole dishes. It can remind you of how many people care about you, and bring you a renewed sense of optimism.

If you share your story online, it can sometimes be difficult to decide how much to write. Should you describe everything you're going through? How personal should you get? Do you need to explain detailed medical information? There is no right or wrong answer to these questions. The information you decide to share will depend on your own comfort level.

Do what feels right for you and your situation. If you are uncomfortable or struggling to decide what to write, take a break. Just remember, the journal is ultimately for you.

BRUCE AND SHARON PEARSON

A Journey and a Gift

They don't give you the truly devastating news over the phone. They told us only that our girls had been in a car accident and that both were critically injured. They were working on one and CAT-scanning the other, and we should come to the hospital right away. Our world spun into crisis mode and we could hardly keep our thoughts straight. Halfway to the hospital we suddenly remembered that our twelve-year-old son, Ben, had been at the same church event with our girls, and at the last minute had decided to ride home with someone else. We detoured to pick him up.

The head nurse met us at the trauma center entrance and ushered us into the family waiting area. We didn't want to search her face for clues about what had happened. We knew it would be harder to look than to look away. When our friends and other family members began to arrive, we gathered together for strength. We waited, our hearts torn, for someone to tell us what had happened. We prayed for information and deliverance.

Thirty minutes later we got the answer. Bethany, our sixteen-year-old; Hannah, our fourteen-year-old; and Hannah's friend

Angie, also fourteen, were on their way to Angie's house for a bonfire after viewing the movie *Chronicles of Narnia* with their church group. Bethany's 1995 Ford Probe fishtailed on a slick road and slid sideways. Coming from the opposite direction, a fast-traveling, full-sized Chevy Z71 pickup truck T-boned Bethany's car on the passenger side. Bethany was in critical condition with a shattered skull and severe brain injury. Angie, who had been in the front passenger seat, needed the Jaws of Life to get her out. Hannah, in the rear passenger seat, took the brunt of the impact and died in the ER. By the time we'd arrived, she'd already been called home to sing with the angels and to sit at Jesus's feet.

After we had time to begin to absorb the situation, a social worker brought memory boxes and forms that we could use to make imprints of Hannah's hands and feet. Also lockets for pieces of Hannah's hair. We had not yet begun to fully comprehend what had happened to our world.

We missed Hannah terribly, but knew she was at peace, with the Lord, so we focused on Bethany in the here-and-now. The social worker said, "Take all the time you need, and when you're ready, call the nursing supervisor and she will escort you upstairs to the pediatric intensive care unit where you can see Bethany." We finally made it up after midnight.

Bethany was a bloody mess. Her skull was cracked from the left ear all the way across her forehead. Her jaw floated free from fractures on both sides. Her lower jawbone was damaged where it connects to the skull, underneath the ears. There was a pool of blood, called a hematoma, in her brain. Her right eye bone was shattered, and a bone fragment rested against her optic nerve, affecting vision in her left eye. A deep gash on the right side of her head had severed the facial nerve. Bethany was heavily sedated and completely unaware, a shell of herself, so very critically injured. We held each other and cried.

We thought we might lose both of our daughters, but the doctors were encouraged by Bethany's stable vital signs despite her injuries. Three ICU nurses hovered, hoping to keep her stable for a massive surgery the next day.

The hospital's chief of neurosurgery performed a craniotomy, removing bone chips, stopping the bleeding, and blotting up the hematoma. Next, a maxillofacial surgeon; an ear, nose, and throat specialist; and a plastic surgeon worked on reconstructing Bethany's face and skull. The procedure took fifteen hours, because, encouraged by Bethany's remaining stable, they'd decided to "go for it," and do as much repair in one surgery as possible. Bethany was wheeled into the recovery room full of titanium staples and plates to remake the bone around her eye, her mandible, and most of the front of her skull. A gap on the top of her head was filled with bone dust, and something called "tissue glue" was used to repair the shredded lining of her skull. A paralyzing agent kept her body at rest. A probe to monitor the skull pressure for excessive swelling stuck out of her brain. A feeding tube ran into her nose. She had a tracheostomy to help her breathe, a chest tube, and a head drain. Her jaw was wired shut and would be for a month. Bethany still leaked a bit of spinal fluid, had minor bruising to her heart, her left pupil was blown, and there was no news about the facial nerve. "Still," the neurosurgeon said, "we accomplished more than we had hoped for."

The details overwhelmed us. We couldn't believe she hadn't also died. The next few days would be critical. Bethany's greatest dangers going forward were strokes, meningitis, more spinal fluid leaks, loss of vision, infection, and brain injury. We prayed for God to spare her from these, to add to the miracle of her survival.

As Bethany lay in the pediatric ICU, she improved day by day in small but significant ways. Worries about bone fractures were eliminated, and tests showed that her arms and legs were responsive, meaning that her spine had been protected. The doctors took her off Propofol paralytic. We allowed anyone who came to visit Bethany to spend time with her. She could hear, and we wanted her to hear words of love and encouragement, but we kept communication at a whisper level so as not to overstimulate her.

One visitor was the firefighter who'd helped Bethany out of her car. Because they were able to extract her the easiest, he'd taken her by ambulance, not helicopter, to Regions Hospital. She was not pinched in like the girls on the other side. As the paramedic worked to get IV lines in Bethany, Rob said he used an Ambu bag to give her 100 percent oxygen with every breath. Because of the extensive injuries to Bethany's face and jaw, the medic wasn't able to get her intubated. "Your girl has a strong right," he told us, explaining that her right arm fought him as he tried to oxygenate her.

That first week was a complete whirlwind. We stayed by Bethany's side and made arrangements for Hannah's burial. So many people were helpful making arrangements for her memorial service so that we could mourn, celebrate her life, and praise the goodness and beauty that Hannah had shared with us every day. Otherwise, much of that time is now an intense blur. We remember flashes of hospital images, the warmth of friends hugging us, the light comfort of feeling supported. Our son, Ben, remembers events much more clearly. He can tell us where each person sat and what they said at a particular time. He may not have had the full capacity to understand how precarious Bethany's situation was, but the moments are indelibly etched into his memory.

We found out about CaringBridge from a friend who had spent the night at the hospital while Bethany was in surgery. He asked for and received our permission to start sites for both Bethany and Hannah. We were too unfocused to post, so he brought a voice recorder and took us to a quiet place for five minutes each day and let us simply speak our minds. Afterward, he or his secretary transcribed the tape and posted the results. Although even these brief interludes were laborious and draining, they were far better than the prospect of having to tell our story over and over again. Now we could update everyone quickly and accurately, according to our perspective.

Hannah's site has only twenty-five posts and is a tribute to her and to the lives she touched. Hannah liked to say, "You don't trash what you value," and she valued people above all. She loved a good story, science, sign language, music, acting, and almost anything she could do outdoors, especially horseback riding and camping. To have her die when it was almost Christmas made it even harder to imagine the hole in our heart ever being filled. We missed her flair and spunk terribly.

We recently got a guest-book message from a woman who worked in the nursery at our church and now lives in Alabama. She wrote that our words had touched her and that although she didn't know us personally, she'd thought of us many times. On both Bethany's and Hannah's sites we were able to share our hearts' pain with the families who couldn't be right there with us at the hospital, and with those who cared no matter what their connection. It was totally therapeutic and, in many ways, cathartic.

About ten days after the accident we finally slept in our own bed at home for the first time. The experience wasn't as difficult as we'd feared. That first night we stayed up late to look at photographs, and then slept like rocks. One morning on the way to the hospital we saw a spectacular sight: two rainbows streaked upward along either side of the brilliant sun. It was awe-inspiring and dazzling and set the tone nicely for the day. Thank You, Lord, for the beauty of creation. What a gift!

Bruce worked for a company whose personnel policy allowed forty hours off after a death in the family. But his supervisors said, "Take as much time as you need." We began to take half-day shifts to be by Bethany's side. At night we crashed, exhausted, held each other, cried. We cried everywhere, often. But we were never angry at God. We don't ask, "What if?" That only leads to misery. Never once did we say, "How dare you?" We *have* asked, "Why?" often, and still do, but we have to trust that it was part of his plan for us. And while we can't always see it, when we look back at the end of our lives—or perhaps tomorrow—we hope to be able to say, "Now we understand. It all makes sense." We do know that we wouldn't have gotten through the calamity without our faith in God. Knowing Him is a peace that we know a lot of other families simply don't have.

It helped our healing process to realize that what we and Ben and Bethany have gone through can give hope to others in their own lives. In adversity, sometimes just comparing oneself to others helps. "Wow, I haven't gone through something like that. I guess I can hang on." It's very human.

Of course nobody chooses this suffering. But if you have it, you have to face it. We're not special, just one of many walking wounded families. Our plight happens to be the result of a tragic car accident. Someone else's is cancer. Or a miscarriage. Or a horrid disease. How do they persevere? How do they keep perspective? It's by realizing what you have instead of what you don't have. It's by realizing that you're not going on the journey alone. We have a tremendous community, from the several hundred families in our church group, to the homeschool group and, because both girls rode ponies, the US Pony Club. Being alone would be unbearable. People *want* to help. The world is not against you. One of CaringBridge's blessings is enabling you to discover how many people surround you, how many care enough to write even two or three sentences of encouragement and support. All those people are on your side. They truly care. They're praying for you, they're rooting for you. You're in their thoughts and prayers. That's huge.

A national horse trainer followed Bethany's site daily. After nine months or so we actually met her. She was really funny. She teasingly reprimanded us: "You are not journaling daily!" as if we had offended her. "You'd better get on the stick," she said. Reading Bethany's journal had become a part of her day, a habit like her morning coffee. When Bethany had a success, it made her day. When Bethany overcame another hurdle in her recovery, it made her feel the same kind of hope. When you see others rise above it, it gives you hope that you can as well.

About six weeks after the accident Bethany began insisting on seeing Hannah. We knew this was coming and had decided to keep it very simple, not saying more than that Hannah had died in the accident. "Hannah's in heaven with Jesus," we said. Bethany handled it much like a young child would. "I'll bet she's giving Him a big hug." Yet because of her short-term-memory loss we had to tell Bethany this news over and over again. But before long, Bethany's doctor told us that she was asking for *more* details about the accident. "That is my major question," Bethany had told him. "I want my parents to patiently, honestly, and fully answer my questions. I know it is a painful subject, and hard for my parents to discuss. I know they are sad and worried, and I don't want to make them sadder. They are incredible parents and I hate to cause them pain. But I know. They are protective of me and maybe don't want to deal with painful issues with me, but I just want them to be honest and not treat me with such carefulness."

We expected the conversation to be harrowing. It wasn't. We shared the painful details openly and answered her questions honestly. She appreciated hearing more about the accident and about Hannah's memorial services. A psychologist and a chaplain were with us, providing support and adding tender words like, "It's okay to cry" and "There is no blame here. It was an accident."

The conversation was positive and healing, yet Bethany has struggled with depression, for a few reasons. Brain injuries have long-term effects. Physically, she's been put back together, but she still feels very broken. She still struggles to overcome the pain of losing her sister and her previous life. We walk that path with her. No one can drive straight if they're always looking in the rearview mirror. We share that message with Bethany. We remind her of what's true: the accident was an *accident* and not her fault, no matter what doubt the voice in her head raises. She is still alive, and that's not a cause for guilt but celebration. She is a wonderful gift to us.

––––––––––––––––

We homeschooled our children. Sharon was the kids' primary teacher until Bethany was in the fifth grade. When we lived in Atlanta, when Bethany was ten, she went to a classroom setting one day a week. They studied Latin and Greek. She started writing papers. She jumped three grade levels that year.

When we moved back to Minnesota, we found YEAH—Youth Educated At Home—an open school academy that offers classes with teachers to supplement homeschooling. The parent is still the teacher, but the kids have the benefit of, for example, learning languages in a group and having lab capabilities for science classes. You get the best of both worlds: the kids get the positive peer support and pressure of being in a classroom one or two days a week, but they do the rest of the work at home.

Bethany would have been bored to death in the public school system. She sat in on veterinary-med-school classes the year before her accident. She was being groomed as a future partner by one of the head med-school instructors. At fifteen, prior to the accident, she was tenth in the nation in her horse knowledge. She was extremely self-confident. There was hardly anything she tackled that she didn't achieve. She was beautiful, vivacious, and maybe, she would even admit, a bit prideful because she was so accomplished. She was larger than life in many ways. Socially adept, she had lead parts in plays. People said, "You're Bethany's parents? Wow, what a delightful kid."

Bethany has always been supremely bright; her accomplishments postaccident prove that. But she's not the same as she once was. Since recovering from the accident, Bethany's been a completely different person. She's still beautiful, but she is much more sensitive. Much more compassionate and caring. Now we see in her many of her sister Hannah's character traits and attributes. Bethany wasn't cold before, but now she's much more willing to be huggy. She knows that she can never re-create who she was, but that doesn't seem to bother her. She says, "God couldn't use me as I was."

Bethany is twenty-three now and still suffers from some short-term-memory issues. She lost four or five months, or more, of memory. CaringBridge is her source of knowledge about what happened. She's read the journal over and over. It's been very hard for her. College is also difficult. She's not writing as much. And yet she won't give up.

We believe that God redeemed Bethany's life for a greater purpose. Even though it's hard, she's got to be okay with, "Okay, Lord, whatever You're willing, I'm working with You." She can fight God and keep saying, "I don't like this! I don't want this! I hate this!" because we all feel that way at times, but it's important to balance those feelings with, "But it's not all about me." You grieve what you've lost every day, but you also have to treasure all you have. It is a miracle that we didn't lose Angie and Bethany too.

Hope that is based in reality can get you through the hard times. Hope is central to a life well lived, to finding the purpose in each new day. When you're in the darkness, you can't see anything. It's very bleak. Hope and faith help you believe a new day will dawn. If you don't have that hope, then you despair. We are on this journey called life and, yes, there are bumps, bruises, high points, low points, hills, and valleys. The last few years were certainly not part of our original plan for our family. But an overflowing love-bucket of kindness and grace continues to be filled by our God, our friends and neighbors, and our family. Life is a journey and a gift.

Bethany is in her third year of college at North Central University, in Minneapolis, working toward a communications degree with an emphasis on public relations. She speaks to high schools and driver's education classes, volunteers with Hope Rides, an organization that connects children with horses, and rides her own horse, Campari. She writes that "finding quality friends is very important, setting aside specific time for studying is vital, maintaining a calendar can only bless you, and clinging to God is the most important thing."

> "Do not think that love in order to be genuine has to be extraordinary. What we need is to love without getting tired. Be faithful in small things because it is in them that your strength lies."
>
> —*Mother Teresa*

ANDY BRIDGE

Doctor, Heal Thyself

I don't think people know how hard it is. They say, "Oh, how's Andy doing? I'm so glad Andy's doing great." I want to say to them, "Yeah, but it's still really hard." His life is difficult. It takes a lot more time to do everything. Getting ready in the morning takes a couple hours. Taking a shower is a big deal. Everything we take for granted. You can't appreciate the gift of mobility that we all have until you have it taken from you.

—Dr. Tom Bridge

I was on top of the world. I'd finished college, gone to medical school, done my internship, completed a very competitive dermatology residency, and was moving north to Chicago to find a job. I had a few options, so I went to the city for an interview and to look for a place to live.

I stayed with a friend in a third-floor walk-up apartment in an old building. The stairs wrapped around a well in the center. I was on the top landing, looking for some keys I'd dropped, when

I went over the low railing, fell thirty feet to the bottom, and landed on my back. That changed some of my plans.

I tried to get up, but couldn't. In fact, I could barely lift my neck to look down at my feet. I thought, *All right, let's try to move the right foot.* Nope. *Okay, let's try the left foot.* Nothing. I could move my arms, so I felt around on my body and realized I could feel some places but not others. Where I did have feeling, the pain was intense. I diagnosed myself in about thirty seconds: I was paralyzed. Later I got the details: I'd crushed two thoracic vertebrae, severed my spinal cord, cracked my head, and broken a few ribs. Thank goodness I'd never lost consciousness.

A guy ran out of an apartment on the ground floor. He said, "Wow, that was the loudest noise I've ever heard." Then he took a close look at me and said, "Whoa, you are really bust up." I said, "Thanks. Could you call nine-one-one for me?" He said, "Sure. Your head's bleeding like crazy, too." I said, "Would you mind grabbing me a towel or something so I can put a little pressure on?" He came back with a towel and then disappeared for a long time. I presumed he was calling 911. I held pressure.

Because my arms worked, I found my phone in my pocket and tried calling several people. I couldn't get ahold of anybody, not even my parents, so I left messages. I think I said, "I took a fall and I'm really messed up. I need some help." I'm amazed at how incredibly lucid I was at the time.

The guy from the apartment didn't come back, so I called 911 myself, then figured out he'd already called when two ambulances arrived. The first EMTs said, "You're too injured for us to take you anywhere." The second set took me to the Illinois Masonic Hospital trauma center for evaluation. During the ride I told them what had happened, and my self-diagnosis, but their attitude was basically, "Yeah, yeah, whatever." They didn't believe me.

My parents didn't hear about my accident until my father got a call at four in the morning from an ER nurse "looking for the father of Andrew Bridge." My dad practices family medicine and is accustomed to being woken in the middle of the night, but he wasn't on call and didn't expect the phone to ring.

The nurse told him that I had a serious spinal injury and couldn't move my legs after a fall down a stairwell—but otherwise I was stable. My dad got my mom up and, as he later told me, said, "We need to pray for Andy. He's been injured." She got pretty emotional.

My father found his cell phone—he'd turned it off—and listened to my message: "Hey Dad, I'm really messed up. I've fallen and I'm really messed up." He told me he could hear the guy from the ground-floor apartment in the background, and my conversation with him. "But I deleted it," he said. "I didn't want to hear that one again."

My parents got dressed and made it to Chicago in two hours.

The conventional wisdom is that doctors make bad patients. In my case, being a new doctor helped. After the ER, I got a bed in the ICU and met with a neurosurgeon. You'd think he'd be able to handle the *whole* nervous system, but the doctor at Illinois Masonic was more of a brain guy, not a spine guy, so he didn't really know what to do. The actual spine surgeons weren't available for another three or four days. I knew enough to convince him that I needed to get out of there and into a better facility. We made some calls and got a recommendation to a top surgeon at Northwestern. I transferred over around midnight of the day after the fall, was prepped for surgery by 6:30 a.m., and was on the operating table around noon.

My parents expected a long surgery, but the operation finished early with good news. The surgeon had realigned my fractured spine and decompressed my spinal canal. I had no leaks of cerebral spinal fluid, so they did not have to place any drains in the sack around my spinal cord. I only had a couple of transfusions. All in all, a very encouraging report.

With my father's help and because of our combined medical knowledge, I was able to advocate for myself. Most others aren't that fortunate, and it points to the need for everyday people to have an advocate who knows medicine or the medical system, because there's so much room for mistakes to be made and for procedures not to be done in a timely manner.

A few days after my surgery, my doctor told me about a clinical trial in which I'd be the first person in the United States to get an embryological stem cell transplant to repair my spine. Less than a week earlier a company had been FDA approved for a trial, and I could have been Patient #1 in the phase-one study. I had a day and a half to decide. I pulled up a bunch of journal articles and talked with some other physicians who knew more about the procedure. Here's where being a doctor paid off again. If I'd had no medical background, I probably would have just said, "Yeah, sure, let's do that."

Instead, my father and I met with my neurosurgeon. He explained that Northwestern was one of twelve sites prepared to do the transplant procedure, and the first to have completed the steps to be officially approved. I met all the specific qualifications: a thoracic spine injury, seven to fourteen days from injury, and so on. Everything fit. My dad was hopeful, because otherwise my prognosis for any significant recovery was grim. But I wanted to know more. I spoke to the chairman of Northwestern's neurology department. He said, "You need to know that I've been quoted in the *New York Times* as being opposed to this trial. I don't think it should go on." He explained why, and my father agreed he made good sense. The chairman's daughter was a spinal-cord-injury patient and, like any of us, wanted to leap at any chance of a recovery, but he said, "I think there will be better trials, better studies. If I were you, I wouldn't do it."

I thought it through and decided that I didn't want to be Patient #1 in a phase-one trial. I made the right choice. The company did four procedures during the next year, abruptly ended the trial, and after fifteen years of being solely in the business of stem cells they got out and focused on nanotechnology.

———

There are many stories on CaringBridge. Some have happy endings, some don't, and some are like mine: a really shitty thing happened, but with the help of great friends, family, a support network, and a positive outlook, you can make the most out of any situation. I knew I could be angry or bury my head in the ground, but neither would make me any better. I also understood the severity of my injury from a relatively early stage. I remember having an MRI for persistent pain in an area where I shouldn't have had any. I met with the neurosurgeon's resident. He'd been in the military and had spent a lot of time in Iraq, so he had seen a lot of spinal cord injuries. He was straightforward with me: "Your spinal cord is devastated." Translation: No room for hope here, buddy. Nothing's gonna come back.

Hearing that, knowing the test results, puts a limit on hope of regaining sensation and motor function. Sometimes even when physicians know the outcome, they equivocate at the outset. Some of the examinations are pretty subjective, so that it is difficult to tell sometimes if the paralysis is complete or incomplete. When I was discharged, they had me as Class B, which means "technically incomplete." But based on the MRI findings, it's actually most likely complete. I had a minor gain of motor function in my abs, and if I'd had the resources or ability to do six months of eight-hours-a-day rehab—there's a place in China where a couple of people have done it—I might have been able to beat my body into re-forming some sort of connection. But I didn't have that luxury.

That's a tough nut to swallow for someone who'd always been very independent. Fortunately, to become a doctor I had to complete years of tasks that required intense focus. As an intern, I'd be on call every third or fourth day, and work 120 hours a week in thirty-hour shifts. Because I was in charge of very sick people, I had to keep slugging through, regardless of whether I wanted to or not. During my first month as an intern I had to pronounce five people dead in the span of four hours. Most of them were patients I didn't know and hadn't spent any time with. I was just covering at night for their regular doctors. That left me to talk to the families and be compassionate, but I also had to find a way to disconnect myself so I didn't go crazy. I believe this intensive and stressful training played a part, after the fall, in my ability to cope with radical changes in my plans at the last second.

I'd just finished ten tough years of postgraduate training. While my buddies were out making money, having fun, and living large, I'd basically given up my twenties. Then, when it was finally my turn to start practicing everything I'd been working toward, to live the good life with the bright lights in the big city, I fell down a stairwell. I had every right to be pissed as hell, at the situation and at the world. But I wasn't. I couldn't even muster anger.

Maybe I'm naturally practical and realistic. Being pissed off wouldn't change anything. I choose not to dwell on the negative. What would be the point? Besides, I'm way too busy learning how to live a new way, and then coping with it, to spare the time. I had rehab to distract me. I had full days. I had to be up early to get breakfast and get dressed, then go through several hours of therapy. I'd maybe have some visitors, then I'd go through the hygiene routine of someone bathing me or doing my bowel prep—which I never wrote about on CaringBridge. These things usually go unspoken. Every day now I have to manually dis-impact my bowels to have a bowel movement. For the first six months to a year, other people had to do it for me. A technician would lube up a glove and…I don't have to draw a picture. I remember being somewhere with my dad and crapping my pants—and we'd have to find a way to take care of it. Shortly after I went back to work, I had to leave because it happened there. The reason: neurogenic bowel, meaning it's sometimes stimulated by the nervous system beyond my control.

I also have neurogenic bladder and wore diapers for twenty months. I'd get infections. I've since had some procedures done to help with incontinence and I've gotten better. But it's a short-term fix, and I'm not sure how long it will last. Any day now I could start pissing my pants again.

CaringBridge allowed me to provide updates and read words of encouragement and support. My father did the original Caring-Bridge post. He knew about it because my junior high science teacher was a friend of the family, went to our church, and was an all-around incredible guy. He developed pancreatic cancer and had a CaringBridge site during the last year and a half of his life. My dad told me that years ago, if you got injured and had to go to the hospital, you got the news out by getting a pocket-ful of dimes and quarters and using the pay phone in the hall. Now, with cell phones, e-mail, and websites like CaringBridge, you can get hundreds of responses in a week.

A year and a half after the accident, on my birthday, I wrote a very honest entry in my CaringBridge journal. I said that I wasn't pessimistic or asking for pity, but the reality of my every day is that I wake up in the morning and I find myself in the same po-sition that I found myself on the night of the injury. Flat on my back. Every night in bed I stare at the same damn feet that don't move. So life is hard and it's not going to get any easier. It sucks. But what's important is that I accept it for what it is.

That was probably the most vulnerable post. I *was* vulnerable. I went to the mall on one of my first trips out of the hospital and I lost it. I cried uncontrollably in a corner of the mall, just from seeing people walking around. Sometimes I'd listen to a certain song and start crying. Existence is a dance. Having family and friends, a community of people who love me and want to do whatever they can to help me through with the emotional and psychological dance, make my life better.

I have great folks. They live about an hour north of Indianapo-lis, where I live now, and it was hard on them to rearrange their lives for a couple of years and constantly be with me in Chicago. But they did it. I'm lucky. My father certainly understands tragic situations and he managed to process mine more quickly than my mother could. She was especially vulnerable because her father had recently passed away, followed by her mother a few months later. If the most unbearable experience for a parent is burying a child, the next toughest has to be seeing him or her suffer and endure extreme hardship.

We all handle our situations differently. The best advice I got about how to live was from a guy named Matthew Sanford. He runs a center in Minnesota, where he works with spinal cord injuries and anybody who's disabled. He's also disabled from a car accident when he was thirteen. He's in his forties now.

I met Matthew through a good friend in Indianapolis who is also disabled. He was walking his dog at night when two guys robbed him for twenty bucks. He gave them the money, turned around, and headed home. They shot him in the lower back. He should have died, but didn't. He invited me to one of Matthew's seminars, which was directed toward yoga instructors. I had never done any yoga and it had only been four months since my fall, so I didn't have great control over my body.

I was too worn out after the first day to go back for the second day, but I wanted to say good-bye to Matthew and thank him. We had a short conversation, during which he told me that the best way to deal with being disabled, with any tragic situation, was this: "You've got to become a veteran. You've got to figure shit out, get through it, and become a veteran of this as fast as you can."

I've since spoken to other people whose injuries are even more acute than mine, and they echo Matthew's advice: Figure out as much as you can on your own and also learn from other people who have been there longer than you have. Get as independent as you can as soon as you can.

I now drive my own van. Recently, my wheelchair wheels weren't locked when I transferred, and it moved, and I fell on the floorboards, in my building's garage—where there's *no cell phone service.* I couldn't reach my keys, and no way would anyone have known I was in the van, let alone on the floor. I asked myself, *Well, what am I gonna do now?*

I lay there for a minute and thought it through, hearing Matthew's advice in my head. I tried one thing and it didn't work. Tried a second thing and that didn't work. Tried a third and managed to get back in the wheelchair. I checked that off my "veteran" list, got out of the van, and went on my way.

Moving through Grief

Grieving is an individual process, but most people experience similar emotions. Psychiatrist Elisabeth Kübler-Ross was the first to identify these common feelings among patients facing a terminal illness, and she subsequently introduced what became known as the "five stages of grief":

Denial: "This can't be happening."

Anger: "Why me? It's not fair. Who or what is to blame?"

Bargaining: "I'll do anything if I can just have more time."

Depression: "I don't care what happens. I'm too sad."

Acceptance: "I can't change this, so I may as well prepare for it."

There is no right or wrong way to grieve, and no path one must follow in order to heal. Grieving is as personal as one's thumbprint. But take note of any extreme feelings, particularly of guilt, anger, or fear. Some emotions, left unchecked, can spiral out of control. Professional counselors can help.

IRELAND KAY MEYER

The New Normal

God blessed us with a little girl.
An angel from above.
God chose a special family for Ireland to love.
She has touched the lives of many.
She is an angel without wings.
God brought her down from heaven to teach us many things.
Her spirit is a strong one.
Her love will never end.
Ireland, our little girl, forever we will love.

Two weeks before our daughter, Ireland, was born, I began to itch. It was an insane sensation all over my body as if my skin had gone crazy. I had no idea why. I couldn't find a rash. I hadn't eaten anything unusual. My only guess was that because my husband, Sean, and I, and our two young boys had just moved into a new house, maybe I'd used a cleaning product that I shouldn't have.

If only it had been that simple. My mom lived right behind us, and she wanted to search for an answer online, so we Googled and Yahoo-ed and finally found what sounded exactly like my condition: cholestasis of pregnancy. According to the Mayo Clinic website, cholestasis "refers to any condition in which the flow of bile, a digestive fluid from the liver, slows or stops. It usually occurs in late pregnancy and triggers intense itching, usually on the hands and feet but sometimes on other parts of the body." The article was, on the one hand, reassuring: the condition could be intensely uncomfortable but posed no long-term risk to the mother. But on the other hand it sounded a big alarm: cholestasis could be dangerous for a developing baby.

My mother insisted that I call my family doctor at home even though it was a Sunday. He wasn't around, so we called the Mayo Clinic instead, and a doctor there sounded concerned. "You need to have a blood test to check your liver enzymes right away." When my general practitioner finally returned my call, he didn't have the same sense of urgency. "Scientifically that sounds very interesting, but I've never seen it. Come in and I'll give you some cortisone cream."

At my appointment the next morning I insisted he do the blood work. A nurse stuck a needle in my arm and filled a couple of vials. He gave me some cortisone cream, too. When I called for the results, the doctor said, "Oh, let me go check on that. But I can tell you right now it's going to be fine."

"Well," he said, when he returned—and I could almost feel him scratching his head, confused, "you *do* have elevated liver enzymes, but I still don't think it's related to your pregnancy or what's causing the itching. But let's look into this further."

He did. Not only did I have cholestasis of pregnancy, but my unborn baby had growth retardation. I also had extra amniotic fluid and no one knew why. Cholestasis meant that Ireland could be stillborn if not delivered between the thirty-sixth and thirty-eighth weeks—which is where I was—so I had an amniocentesis. The results revealed that her lungs weren't developed enough to deliver. They scheduled another amnio, but without warning I went into labor on my own.

Ireland arrived on December 15, 2007, at 12:28 p.m., in Mankato, Minnesota, which is about ninety minutes south of the Twin Cities: Minneapolis and Saint Paul. She weighed five pounds and seven ounces, and was nineteen inches long. It was a joyful occasion, marred only by Ireland's being so immediately and obviously sick that she had to be airlifted to another hospital. There, the doctors discovered an enormous challenge she'd be lucky to overcome.

Ireland had esophageal atresia, which means that her esophageal tube didn't attach to her stomach because it hadn't developed completely. Instead, her esophagus ended as a pouch in her upper chest. She also had an atrial septal defect, which is a fancy name for a hole in the heart, and a bicuspid aortic valve, which refers to the leaflets of the aortic valve. This is the valve that leads out of the heart to the aorta, the big blood vessel that delivers oxygen-rich blood to the body. Normally, the aortic valve has three leaflets. A bicuspid valve has only two leaflets. Neither of the heart defects were much of an issue at the time.

Ireland also had Down syndrome.

When Ireland was only two days old, she had surgery to put a gastric tube into her stomach so that she could eat. She did really well, and they were able to take her off the ventilator and even give her a "tanning session," since she was a bit jaundiced. But the huge problem remained, and the doctors said they wouldn't be able to connect what there was of her esophagus to her stomach until she got bigger.

As a family we also had to grow new connections as we left our old lives behind. We couldn't anticipate the wild ride, and in many ways I'm grateful that we couldn't know the future then. In retrospect, I think of that time as the beginning of a nonstop roller-coaster ride, with us gripping the safety bars and hanging on for dear life. We called it the "new normal."

At first, Ireland stayed in the hospital, in an incubator bubble, bravely bearing a relentless series of procedures. We celebrated Christmas there with our little angel, who wore a little holiday outfit brought by one of her nurses. She looked so cute. She had lots of visitors and got a stocking-full of goodies as well. The gift to us was prayers and support, which we sorely needed. We appreciated it beyond words.

As Ireland got stronger day by day, she got to meet her brothers, Deven, who was ten, and Wesley, who was three. Despite her troubles, Ireland was, even then, such a joy-filled child. Her smile was incandescent and almost indelible. The boys and Ireland took to each other immediately.

Meanwhile, Sean and I met constantly with the doctors, who monitored the growth of Ireland's stomach as we silently wished it to inch up, closer to where her esophagus ended. We met with a geneticist and cardiologist who told us about the different types of Down syndrome. Ireland has trisomy 21, which is the most common kind. We were trained in how to use a home monitor. We learned infant CPR. We got a feeding pump and suction device that we'd use with Ireland when we finally got her home.

When Ireland came home in early January, we were both overjoyed and frustrated. And scared. All with good reason. The reality hit Sean and me that bringing up Ireland would be much more work than we'd anticipated. We floundered, out of our depth. One day Ireland would make gagging and choking noises because her suction machine couldn't keep up with her secretions—which were worse when she had a mild cold. Some days we had to force ourselves not to throw the feeding pump out the window because we couldn't get it to work right. And Ireland came with so much equipment that even a trip to the doctor required two people to take her.

Other days, she'd lie in her crib, radiating love, lighting up our lives. One immediate plus: she quickly figured out her days and nights so that Sean and I could get some sleep, and when she was awake, she was usually cheerful. We felt blessed to have a very contented baby. We vowed to hang in and remain positive that she would get better after her restorative surgery. One day Ireland would be doing fabulous.

Part of what helped us with the ups and downs was the CaringBridge site my cousin set up for me. I hadn't heard about it, and even after I began to post, I didn't tell that many people about it. Writing was a way to deal with *my* anxiety, but pretty quickly one person who read Ireland's journal told another person, who told another person, and suddenly the guest book began to fill up with friends, family, and strangers offering prayers for Ireland and the family and wanting to know how she was doing. That was such a gift. I was so grateful I didn't have to constantly make calls to keep everyone updated on all the twists and turns of Ireland's struggle. I could never have kept up.

Sometimes I didn't want to write, because there were too many facts and figures to get straight, and it was tough enough dealing with real life. I didn't want to relive it. So I just told myself that it was okay to tell everyone about our struggles without going into all the gory details.

We were all so hopeful when Ireland finally went back to the hospital in March to have her esophagus connected. She'd gained weight and gotten much stronger. But when the doctors measured the gap, they discovered it was larger than anticipated. That should have been the end of it, but then they tried a smaller measuring rod and said the gap looked better. The surgery was on.

A two-hour procedure ended up taking four and a half hours. Sean and I were beyond antsy. I drove him nuts by pacing around the waiting room, while he played Nintendo and read a Lightning McQueen children's book. I guess we all have our ways of dealing with stressful situations!

Finally the doctor came out to tell us the news. What the surgeons had anticipated, on the second measurement, to be a 1.5- to 2-inch gap, turned out to be a 4.5- to 5-inch gap. What they thought was the other end of her esophagus on the X-ray was actually her stomach being pushed up with the metal rod. Luckily, he said, his senior surgical partner was in the operating room and they were able to cut around the muscle of Ireland's esophagus and pull it far enough down (like a Slinky) to stitch the two ends together. They also had to move her stomach up a little, and would put her on Zantac because she would have reflux. "It was the best thing for Ireland," he said, trying to reassure us. "If we'd quit the procedure in the midst of it, the ends of her esophagus would have formed scar tissue and would have stopped growing." The surgeon added that he had never ever seen such a big gap be able to come together.

We were overjoyed, and yet depressed. When we finally got to see Ireland at 7:30 that evening, we couldn't even pick her up. She was attached to a ventilator, and she'd been paralyzed medically so there was no chance of movement that could cause the stitches to rip apart. They had put a central line into Ireland's neck to allow medication to be given and blood withdrawn without having to poke her all the time. She handled it well. So did I. Sean had to go into another room.

Ireland hung in there, every day amazing us more and more. She was only three months old. Clearly our little princess was a fighter.

Those who loved Ireland did their part in the fight as well. Two days after her surgery, they staged a benefit full of love and support. When we left Ireland to attend the benefit, she looked pale, but we went anyway. While we were away, Ireland had complications. Her hemoglobin levels dropped very low and she had to have a blood transfusion. Then her blood wasn't clotting fast enough, so they gave her plasma. By the time we got back to the hospital, she was, thankfully, no longer pale and we tried not to beat ourselves up too much for leaving.

Unfortunately that episode was just the beginning. March had come in like a lamb but was about to go out like a lion. On March 18, the doctors found an air pocket in Ireland's chest and possibly an air leak, so they hooked her chest tube back up to suction. They switched her to a different diuretic, again hoping to help rid her of some of the fluid she'd accumulated and was storing—just where, they didn't know. Her hemoglobin levels began to fluctuate again, which meant another transfusion, and she remained on the ventilator. Eventually, the doctors stopped the paralyzing medication, and she opened her eyes once in a while.

A CT scan the next day revealed more bad news: fluid around her lungs and in her chest, necessitating surgery. That's when they discovered that her esophagus and stomach had separated after all—and that the tissue was too inflamed to reattach it. She had a partially collapsed right lung containing fluid, and our little fighter was riddled with infection. All we could do was be full of worry and pray that she would make it through the next few days without developing pneumonia.

We scheduled a talk with the surgeons to discuss next steps, and we ended up transferring Ireland to the University of Minnesota Medical Center, where we met with a surgeon who specialized in long-gap esophageal-atresia repair. Three days later she spent five hours in surgery, and her new surgeon said she was quite a mess. He'd found a "horrible infection" in her chest cavity, "right up there with the worst" he'd ever seen. He cleaned her out, flushed the area, put in four new chest tubes—two small ones pumping in antibiotics, two larger ones pumping out the infection. She was also on IV antibiotics and an antifungal. The next day they added another antibiotic, because they found another kind of bacteria growing. She got a drain in one of her old chest-tube sites. The surgeon closed a hole in Ireland's trachea with a couple of stitches and some glue. He did the same in her thoracic duct, cleaned up other stitches from previous surgeries, and applied traction sutures on the bottom end of her esophagus to stop a leak.

We wondered how she could take it and survive. Still, she persevered.

Afterward the surgeon told us that when Ireland was ready, he would start the growing and stretching process on her esophagus again. But he was uncertain about Ireland's prognosis, because she'd lost about 2 centimeters of esophagus due to the separation. "Right now we'll just focus on her getting over the infection. It will probably take weeks."

Through it all, Ireland continued to amaze us. She fought off two more types of bacteria and a yeast infection. She overcame pneumonia. Finally, the stuff coming out of her chest tubes began to clear up.

Ireland was a little miracle.

I could fill pages and pages with stories of medical procedures, with Ireland's ups and downs, with successes and disappointments, with our struggles to stay close as a family and the bravery with which Ireland's brothers handled not getting enough of Sean's and my attention. It's now been five years of saying "this too shall pass," over and over, from one complication to another, from victory to setback to victory. We've gone to so many doctors over the years. They always say, "Ireland is a very complex case."

Yes, we get that.

But here's the bottom line: Ireland's esophagus is still not attached to her stomach. She still eats through a feeding tube. She still doesn't speak because of damage to the laryngeal nerve during one of her many operations.

Even though in addition to her atresia, Ireland has Down syndrome, we consider that the least of our concerns. There is something so special about her that I would take another Down syndrome child in a heartbeat. I don't even think of it as a medical problem. Ireland is a joy, the bravest little girl that could be. We are happy for every moment with her.

When Ireland was born, the on-call doctor took Sean and me aside and said, "This is either going to make your relationship or break it."

We didn't know how to respond in that moment, but later we took his advice as a challenge. We got through the first year, and the second. Then we had rough patches. At one point I was up in the Twin Cities with Ireland for such a long time that it was almost as if Sean and I were separated for a year. He worked Monday through Thursday and then would visit. I could tell it was very difficult for him to be away, but I was often so overwhelmed by everything with Ireland that when he was there, I just wanted a break. We didn't really fight, but it wasn't unusual for me to take out my frustrations on him. We were both under a lot of stress, and it showed. He couldn't wait to leave and I couldn't wait for him to leave.

Eventually we decided to try therapy, and I'm glad we did. It helped a lot. You always have to work at a marriage. I finally realized that Sean *never* wanted to leave. He would offer to take time off work, and I would have appreciated the help, but we couldn't have him not working either. So I got jealous and upset, thinking he worked and got to come home and relax. In reality, he'd be worried sick about us, and lonely. Once we figured out where each other was coming from, it was better. Now we feel as if we can get through anything.

We have all been home again more or less since last December. It's still tough. What's weird is that some people, now that we're at home and not constantly rushing Ireland off to the hospital for emergencies, think that everything's okay again.

Not so. Our lives are still so crazy. Every week Ireland goes under anesthesia to have a fistula catheter changed out, and that doesn't always go as smoothly as we would like. There are also weekly therapy visits, home visits from the school district, doctor's appointments, and trying to balance the needs of our other kids on top of everything. My phone rings nonstop sometimes: doctors, home health care, insurance companies. I used to be a dental assistant working for my father. For the past five years I've been much busier.

Ireland's dad is a maintenance mechanic, and we're fortunate to have good insurance through his work. We're lucky that right before Ireland was born, a law was passed removing the lifetime-maximum cap, because Ireland is only five and has almost reached the previous lifetime max. Had that been in effect, Ireland would have had to go straight to Medical Assistance, where the level of care is not the same.

Ireland's surgeon really loves her and promised to fix her no matter what, but he's only human and he hasn't been able to yet. So our biggest challenge is to put a plan in place for Ireland. We desperately need one. We ask ourselves every day, *If they can't grow her esophagus, what are we going to do?* We've been told again and again, "one more time" and then it'll connect, but that means she'll have to be in the ICU, in a medically induced coma, and we can't hold her or pick her up. You'd think we'd be used to it, but the routine gets harder every time, because, well, she's not a baby anymore. She's a real person. We've spent five years learning about who she is. When Ireland was a new baby, it would have been the most heartbreaking thing if she didn't make it. But after five years there's so much more love for Ireland, and so much more intimacy, there's interacting with someone who can do the same with you. If something were to happen now, we would be devastated in ways we can't imagine. We *know* her now.

Unfortunately, it seems as if Ireland's very capable doctors are out of options. An ICU doctor who's worked with her many, many times, said, "I hate to tell you this, but I think we're at the point where there's nothing more we can do for her."

The surgeon who changes out her fistula tubes said, "I hate to be the bearer of bad news, but Ireland can't live like this forever. She's going to end up dying."

I know that, but how do you deal with that? I can't accept that, but I can't help wondering if the doctors are secretly thinking, *Enough is enough.*

Sometimes I think about when Ireland was brand-new, before the doctors attempted to put her esophagus together. She had a tiny tube that went into her mouth. Sean and I thought that was the most horrible, awful thing. But if that was all she had now, we'd be grateful.

I know it can always get worse, but I'll never stop fighting for Ireland.

Ireland has taught me the true meaning of life. Every day I'm with this adorable little girl, I reflect on her amazing strength. She inspires me. She's always so happy, even though we sometimes have to do horrible, painful things to keep her alive. Afterward she always gives me a hug and a kiss, as if to console *me*, as if to say that she still loves *me* despite what we've had to put her through.

Sometimes I think God chose our family for Ireland way before we ever thought about having her. I know that because she has touched so many people through CaringBridge and in other ways. Even doctors have told me they've learned things from Ireland. That little girl has more strength than you could ever imagine. What she has gone through and the spirit of life that is in her is absolutely amazing. People are always so drawn to her. There's no better proof of that than the guest book on CaringBridge.

I keep a saying hanging on the wall in our house: "Life isn't about waiting for the storm to pass....It's about learning to dance in the rain."

That's our life with Ireland! I plan on getting that quote tattooed on my leg along with Ireland's handprint someday.

I feel so blessed that I am her mom.

Messages of Hope

Many friends and family members send cards or tack up "Welcome Home" banners, but for a twist on the typical greeting, try a chalk message. Keep in mind that you don't need to be an artist for this caring craft to be meaningful—it's the gesture that counts. Like a giant greeting card, decorating a driveway or walkway with heartfelt messages of inspiration promotes joy. Imagine arriving home after a hospital stay and discovering a special message. Children will especially appreciate this kind of greeting. And it's environmentally friendly!

So grab a quotation from a book or a poem, draw upon your friend's favorite movies or television shows, or stick with tried-and-true messages of love and support:

You are Loved

You are Radiant

May the Force Be with You

To create your own sidewalk greeting card, gather plenty of sidewalk chalk and a friend or two to help out (depending on just how big you want to go).

Find out when the family will be away. Your greeting will have more impact if it's a surprise. Also, check the weather. You don't want your message to be washed away by rain before they get to see it.

Bring a sketch with you. It's easier to draw a large image if you plan ahead. This gives you time to think about how the words will fit on their driveway or sidewalk and what colors you would like to use. Additionally, if you enlist helpers, having a sketch makes it easier to share directions.

Don't forget to take a picture before you leave. Post it on your Facebook page and tag your loved one so others can add their own messages of support. You might also inspire others to create one for someone else!

PAUL HAIN AND KATHY KURTH

Everything Happens for a Reason

PAUL HAIN: I've had multiple careers. I tried my hand at professional photography, and I worked for my father as a commercial artist. One day he asked what I really wanted to do and I said, "Teach." He gave me his blessing. I got a scholarship to the Chicago Academy of Fine Arts. First I worked as an art teacher for six years, then an administrator, and finally a principal for twenty-four years. On my summers off, I worked with my superintendent to computerize the school district. I'd been trained in computers to get my first master's degree, and then got a second in school finance. Soon I was a business manager for the district.

I was working on my doctorate when I was diagnosed with ulcerative colitis (UC). With UC, your colon becomes inflamed and you have major problems with diarrhea, blood, and mucus. It's a horror story. The doctors thought I might need to have some of my large intestine removed, but they opted to try steroid therapy instead. It took thirteen months, but I healed. The doctors noted that my liver enzymes were elevated, but they said that wasn't uncommon when someone has a major intestinal problem.

Five years later, during a routine checkup, my doctor said my gallbladder was filled with large stones. I'd never had a gallstone attack, and I asked him how it was possible. He wasn't sure, but he was sure I needed to have my gallbladder removed because if even one of the stones tried to pass through, it was going to hurt like hell and be complicated by the colitis.

After the operation, the surgeon spoke to my wife, Dee. "Is your husband a drinker?" he asked.

"Paul? What? No way. He never drank alcohol in his life."

"Well, somehow he's got stage-three liver cirrhosis," he said. "I've never seen this unless somebody's been an alcoholic."

We knew I had intestinal scarring from the ulcerative colitis and that my liver enzymes had been high, but cirrhosis was something new.

I kept having problems. In 2006, an old infant hernia finally pushed through just below my belly button. After it was repaired, and an internist was reviewing the X-ray to make sure that the Kevlar pad had knit smoothly in place, he noticed that my spleen was enlarged. He wanted to refer me to my gastroenterologist for follow-up.

So I had a large spleen. Everyone knows that you can live without a spleen, so I asked if I should just get it taken out. "This is beyond my expertise," he said, and sent me to a specialist at Froedtert Hospital in Milwaukee, an hour away.

Dee and I went for my appointment believing that we'd be told what I already thought I knew: I had an enlarged spleen and it would be best to remove it. But when we walked into the meeting, instead of one doctor, we saw five doctors seated around a table. Their first words: "Dr. Hain, we'd like to welcome you to our liver transplant program."

I was stunned. "Did you say 'transplant'?" They had, and they went on to explain in precise detail that I had primary sclerosing cholangitis (PSC). A couple of moments later I couldn't have remembered that name if you paid me. I was still reeling from the shock. But I managed to ask the important questions: "What about this disease? How do you treat it?"

"We can treat the symptoms and perhaps slow its progression, but the only cure is a liver transplant."

It felt like I must have done something wrong and that my incurable illness was a penalty exacted by God. I had to work through a mental movie of my whole life to realize that I didn't have anything to feel bad or guilty about. God is good, I decided. God created us in His image and likeness. It stood to reason, then, that the perfect man or woman of God's creating did not include diseases or imperfection. In reality, God knew me as He created me, and it was only my limited, mortal view of spiritual life that was making me think that something human could change God's creation or my relationship to God. Once I realized that, I was able to focus on what needed to be done physically.

I asked the doctors how I'd gotten PSC. They said it was most likely genetic and linked to the development of my autoimmune system when I was an infant. In other words, the disease might have been triggered by a bacterial infection at a time when my immune system wasn't fully developed, so eventually my system began to attack my own organs because it didn't know how to turn on and turn off at the appropriate times.

Normally, if you get a cold, your lymph nodes swell up under your jaw and elsewhere. In my case, my lymph nodes would swell up and there wouldn't be anything going on. No cold, no nothing. Now my immune system was flooding my liver with unwanted white cells and was slowly killing it. What's more, all those diseases and problems I'd had—ulcerative colitis, gallstones, cirrhosis—weren't stand-alone issues. According to my team of doctors they were *all* caused by the underlying primary sclerosing cholangitis.

PSC's cause is still unknown, but medical science does know the mechanism of the disease: the immune system goes out of control, causing excess bile to back up in the liver. Bile is a powerful toxin that leads to cirrhosis, the permanent destruction of the liver cells. PSC is extremely rare. So much so that doctors who do know about it only learned from a textbook or were told about it by a teacher.

Despite the diagnosis, I felt quite healthy, so I remained positive about my circumstance. In fact, I sometimes felt so wonderful that from office visit to office visit with the hepatologist (a doctor who specializes in the diseases of the liver), I almost expected him to say, "You know, Paul, we made a mistake. You don't have this." I wasn't yellow, and I didn't itch. I hadn't lost any muscle mass. I was fit as a fiddle, yet I had PSC. At the time of my final diagnosis, my cirrhosis had progressed to end-stage 4. I asked the doctor to explain that. "Occasionally, people with PSC—and there aren't many of you, maybe four or five hundred in the country—are asymptomatic."

I persisted. "Could you be mistaken? Could the liver enzymes be elevated just because of the ulcerative colitis?"

"No, there's no mistake. We've taken liver biopsies. We've looked at the cell structure under the microscope. This cirrhosis is an exact pattern match with PSC."

What could I say? I was at a good teaching hospital. Their

research was not a hit-or-miss proposition, where they looked up stuff on the Internet or sourced diagnoses out of ten-year-old medical texts. "It's wonderful that you're asymptomatic," my doctor cautioned, "but don't expect it to continue forever."

My condition was a challenge—like many in life—and I'd meet it, defeat it, and move past it. Eventually I'd get a new liver, and I'd be fine.

———

True to my doctor's prediction, two years later I began to manifest symptoms. I went into liver failure every four to six weeks. While I was hospitalized with one of my numerous battles, a young hepatologist kept waking me up during the night to ask me questions. I really didn't mind, I wasn't sleeping anyway. I learned that he had been told that he would never see a real, live PSC patient, so he wanted to satisfy his curiosity. Fine. That was way better than him seeing a real, dead PSC patient, in my humble opinion.

I was put on the transplant list to receive a donated liver from a cadaver: someone who had just died. But I didn't stay on that list. Whenever I'd have to be hospitalized, I'd get steroids and a broad spectrum of antibiotics, and then I'd bounce back. Sometimes I'd be released after only two days. This was good news in the short run, but bad in the long run.

The United Network for Organ Sharing is a nationwide control group that allocates organs using a scientifically driven method called the Model for End-Stage Liver Disease (MELD). I was told at Froedtert Hospital, where they only performed cadaver transplants, that they would like me to register not only in Milwaukee but in Madison as well, so that I would be listed in two regions and thus increase my likelihood of getting a transplant when I needed one. The number you need in order to determine your eligibility and get a transplant is a MELD score. The hospital in Milwaukee required a 23. In Madison I only needed a 22. During liver-failure episodes, one's MELD number generally rises quickly to 25 or even 35, confirmation that the doctors should actively seek a new liver. My problem was that I'd go into liver failure and I'd stay at 11. I was in serious trouble, but my score didn't show it. "Primary sclerosing cholangitis does not follow the normal progression of liver disease," my Wisconsin doctor explained. "You will die before you get a cadaver transplant."

He proposed a solution. "Paul, you need to work on finding a live donor."

If I'd been surprised to learn that I needed a transplant two years earlier, this news floored me. A live donor? How do you even begin to do that? I'd had a hard enough time adapting to the idea that somebody had to die in an accident for me to get a cadaver liver—but I had come to accept that. Death is going to happen anyway, and that organ might as well be used. If it's to help me, well, that's its purpose.

Now the whole game had changed. I would have to find some way to ask a *living, healthy* person to go through major surgery they didn't need, to give me a piece of their perfectly healthy liver. The procedure was ingenious. The liver has a big lobe and a small lobe. A live-transplant procedure leaves the donor's small lobe untouched and requires two-thirds of the big lobe. The big lobe grows back eventually, but the recovery time isn't easy. A donor remains in the hospital for up to a week, and then there's another month or more of rest at home. Not many people are willing to make that kind of sacrifice.

Frankly, I had to pray a lot.

My wife, Dee, is a teacher, and one day in the lounge at school, a teacher who'd heard I had PSC said, "I think that's what my brother-in-law has." Dee said, "Maybe you're mistaken. It's really rare."

But Dee's friend was correct. He lived in a suburb about thirty minutes away. He wanted to talk, so we got on the phone. He was a year younger than I am, but we'd gone to the same high school, and we grew up only a mile from each other. We'd both been told that our disease had started when we were very young, but our experience suggested another theory. Perhaps our PSC was environmental. We compared notes. What did we do in common that could have triggered it? All we could think of was that in our high school the rooms weren't air-conditioned, so the windows were open and the wind blowing in from the west always carried a god-awful smell from a nearby foundry. For four years we sucked it up daily. The Environmental Protection Agency closed the plant in 1992 because of its air pollution. Maybe that was the culprit?

My new friend told me that he'd had a live-donor transplant six months earlier. His daughter was his donor.

My family is very small and my daughter, Heather, who is the most important thing in my life, is my only child. She and I had the same blood type, but the donor liver also has to physically match up to the sites of the recipient's bile duct, hepatic artery, and the portal vein. Heather wasn't a match.

I had a nephew in Bahrain, who shared my blood type. But he had three toddlers, and the hospital strongly discouraged him, saying, "The risk is very, very low that you'll have any complications from being a donor, but still there is risk. You've got three little babies and you live half a world away."

A friend went for testing, but wasn't compatible. I couldn't just run an ad in the newspaper. I was running out of options.

Heather used Facebook and other social media to get the word out that I needed a live donor. She also posted stories I had written about my disease.

It worked. Kathy Kurth, a high school friend of Heather's, who hadn't seen her since graduation fifteen years earlier, read Heather's Facebook posts and reached out.

KATHY: Life was going wrong for me. Bad things were happening, and I didn't know why. I worked in human resources for an insurance company in Madison, Wisconsin. My husband had gotten a job in central Wisconsin, so we were moving and I planned to transfer to our office in Wausau.

For seven and a half years I'd worked hard. I always got great performance reviews. I had seen plenty of people transfer internally without incident, and even if I couldn't keep my same job, I was confident that I could find another one with the company. But there was an unexpected twist. My boss decided that she didn't want to allow me to transfer outside of my division. My teammates lobbied on my behalf for months, but at the end of the day my boss decided she didn't need me, and my company didn't need me either.

I was heartbroken. I kept telling my husband, "I don't understand why this is happening." I had imagined I'd be driving down to Madison once a month, working in the main office, so I'd keep in touch with all of my friends at work. Instead, everything was collapsing. And yet, in the midst of my unhappiness, I told a good friend in the office, "I know it's all happening for a reason. I just wish someone would give me a road map." He told me, "God has a plan for you. Sometimes we just have to be patient."

That's when I saw some of Heather's comments on Facebook

about her dad needing a liver transplant and the testing. I kept an eye on their progress as people got tested and were ruled out. I decided to e-mail Heather. I told her about losing my job. I wrote, "I just have this weird feeling that maybe I'm supposed to be helping *you guys* right now." It wasn't a question. I knew from the posts that I was the right blood type. I was healthy. I had no children. Plus, Heather and I were close in high school, and back then her parents had always been great to me. If nothing else, I knew I at least had to get tested.

First, I did a lot of research in order to thoroughly understand what I might be getting into. The more stories I read about the live-donor-transplant procedure, the more I believed it explained why everything had happened to me. I *must* be the match. It was part of the plan.

The hospital at Northwestern in Chicago only did testing every other Thursday. They also conducted an extensive review process to make sure potential donors truly understood the risks. You meet social workers. Psychiatrists examine you. You even talk to a financial specialist.

I went for my test the week after Christmas. The surgeon quizzed me to see what I knew about Paul's condition and organ donation. He wanted to know this wasn't something I just thought would be fun to do. I got a battery of blood tests, a physical, and an MRI to determine whether the volume, size, and placement of the veins and arteries of my liver would be compatible.

By the end of the day I was exhausted yet hopeful. I really wanted to be a match, because I felt like being part of the solution would make everything that had happened at work okay. However, I hadn't told anyone in my family about my plan. I was afraid that they would try to talk me out of it. Only Heather and her parents knew. If I was a match, I'd deal with all that. If I wasn't, then my family would not have had to needlessly worry.

The surgical nurse who coordinates the donors gave me the news: I was a match. "But you can still say no," she said. "Paul and Heather don't know yet. You can still back out. If you do, all we'll tell Paul is that you weren't compatible." They did a great job of making me feel comfortable that I could change my mind and not be exposed, but I had no intention of backing out.

I talked with my husband, Pete, and he supported me unconditionally. Now I *had* to tell my parents. I expected to hear them say, "This is crazy. What are you doing? You're a *healthy* person, and you want to have totally unnecessary surgery? You're putting your life at risk."

I confess that I felt a little bit anxious and reckless as I drove to the Illinois suburb where my parents lived to tell them in person. When I finished, I searched their faces for a reaction. To my surprise and relief they agreed. Despite being nervous, they knew that I believed being a donor was something that I needed to do—and they weren't going to be able to talk me out of it.

I called Heather and told her, and that's when it finally hit me that this was real. I felt amazing.

PAUL: As the year drew to a close, I had hoped I could make it through Christmas. I had begun to feel atypically bad. I'd have good days and then I'd have horrible days. The tide had turned against me. I had lost most of my muscle mass. My skin sagged. I looked like a drained chicken. When Kathy was declared a match, I finally felt hope. Soon after getting the news, we met Kathy for lunch at her parents' home. She looked just like she did when she was in high school. She had the same happy smile, sense of humor, confidence. Kathy's husband was also on board. He knew that she wanted to do this, that the chance of harming her was tiny, and that her generosity would mean a new life for me. If Kathy worried that something might go wrong, she never let on. Instead, she radiated faith that everything would work out for both of us. But I had to ask the obvious question: why did she want to donate a piece of her liver? I found it impossible to argue with her answer: "I just knew in my heart this was the right thing to do," she said.

I very much wanted to live, but I felt protective of her. I didn't want her to put herself at any risk for me, so I asked and asked again, "Are you sure you want to do this?" She said she was. That was about as far as I went to discourage her. Believe me, if I had seen any doubt in her face, any at all, I would've said, "Why don't we put it off and you think about this for a while." But that never happened. Kathy was so intensely convinced this was the right thing for her to do that it finally put my trepidations to rest.

KATHY: I know that Paul was initially resistant to the idea of my being a donor. He did not want to impose, and he felt that his need was the ultimate imposition—putting someone else at risk to save his own life. There were plenty of times when...I wouldn't say he tried to talk me out of it, but he tried to talk sense into me. Other times he'd repeat, "It's so selfless." I realize why someone outside of my head might have trouble understanding my motivation, but it wasn't selfless to me. I needed something to make sense of all of the bad things that had just happened to me, of all the uprooting in my life. Because of all that had happened I had completely lost faith and trust in people, and this was, in a sense, the answer to *my* prayers. It fit. It made me feel like no matter what else happened, I was here for a reason. I just couldn't find the words to explain to Paul that my wanting to help him was saving me as much as it was saving him.

PAUL: Depending on your body size, the typical liver is somewhere between eight and eleven pounds. It's the largest organ in your body. It stretches across from your right side to your left, and it tapers down as it goes to your left side. There are two lobes. They take two-thirds of the large lobe as the graft that they implant. In Kathy's case she would survive on the small lobe, which is untouched by surgery, plus 40 percent of the remaining large lobe, which would regenerate.

The liver is the only organ in the body besides the skin that regenerates itself. When we were all healed and recovered, we would both have full-sized, fully functioning livers.

Just to be on the safe side, and to ease any concerns, the surgeon explained to both of us that only once in the United States, in Colorado, has a live donor died on the table. They weren't able to explain why, except that it wasn't as a result of the organ being removed.

Paul and Kathy went in separately to surgery before 7:00 a.m., on February 8, 2012. Paul's liver was removed, and the surgeons dissected Kathy's for the transplant. Kathy was sewn up and sent to recovery around 1:00 p.m. Then the doctors began the delicate task of connecting the new section of liver to Paul. He emerged from surgery at 5:00 p.m. Both had done well.

PAUL: I became conscious about eighteen hours after surgery and found myself in intensive care, where a nurse sits by your bedside twenty-four hours a day. I had five tubes running through my jugular and down into various organs. I also had a breathing tube down my throat and a gastric tube down my nose. Fortunately I knew to expect that when I came to, but as soon as my eyes opened, I could feel myself fighting against the gag response. I had to steady myself to not panic.

The nurse leaned in and said gently in my ear, "Paul, you're awake. You're attempting to breathe on your own. That's a very good sign. I'll get the doctor. We'll remove that tube from you in just a few minutes, so just be patient." I struggled and tried not to choke, and managed to hold it off.

Once the tube was out, my first thought was about Kathy. I needed to know how she was. It wasn't very long until Pete, her husband, wheeled her in.

She looked like an angel, even in a hospital gown. She was smiling as always. She reached out her hand and held mine. Simply her warmth brought me immediate comfort. And tears. They told me that she'd been up and walking already. I was still groggy, but we talked for a while.

After Kathy left, between sleep and consciousness, I realized over and over that Kathy had given me the gift of life, the most precious gift I could ever receive. I asked myself if I would ever be able to put myself in Kathy's place and give the gift to another. I believe that having been on the receiving end made it easy for me to know in my heart that I could do it too.

Kathy and I eventually moved out of the hospital to a recuperative residence hotel very close by. We'd see each other at the continental breakfast. She showed me her scar, an incision about four inches long. Mine looks like a peace sign that runs from the belly button, over to the right side and up to my sternum, and then down the left side back to the belly button. When we were finally able to hug, we both knew we were going to make it. In a way, we share the same blood now. I feel as close to her as to a much-loved relative. A piece of Kathy is keeping me alive, and that's a great feeling.

KATHY: When I visited Paul at the hotel where we were sent to rehabilitate after being discharged from the hospital,

I felt shy and awkward. Maybe it was because he was so obviously overwhelmed with emotion and he couldn't find the words to say anything. In fact, I was embarrassed that I had made him feel like that. I was uncomfortable because he was so uncomfortable. It's understandable. Our experience was intimate in a way most people will never experience. What helps is that we both have a sense of humor. For instance, the surgical staff had taken pictures of his original liver and of the piece of mine. Paul e-mailed me to say, "I want to post these on CaringBridge. I want people to see the difference. But since it's your liver, I want your permission."

"It isn't my liver anymore," I replied. "You can do what you want with it!"

PAUL: Whenever we get together now, I call it a liver reunion.

KATHY: I had suggested CaringBridge to Heather because I had a coworker whose wife had colon cancer and he had used CaringBridge to keep family and friends updated on her progress. I remember him saying how he would read the guest book to her every day and that when she was really feeling down after chemo, it helped raise her spirits. I said, "Heather, I've seen this. I've used it as a guest, and I think it's the perfect fit."

Then I drove back to Wisconsin from Illinois, and by the time I got home and logged onto my computer, she already had the site set up. She was so excited about it that she put pictures up and filled things in.

Later, when I had very little recollection of the first two days after surgery, I relied on the CaringBridge journal as the record of what had happened. I read through it when I was finally off the medication and my vision was back to normal.

I've been so deeply impressed with how social media has expanded the reach of support and prayers! It's pretty incredible to

250

see how many people have written, "We added you to our prayer list at church or work or school." I know CaringBridge made a huge difference in my recovery, and I'm so grateful for that.

It strikes me that the CaringBridge sites have the power to do so much good just by uniting so much positive energy in one focused place. Even when the news isn't glowing, it helps the patient and their family to feel connected and supported, to remember they're not alone, and that there are so many people in the world thinking of them and caring for them.

PAUL: I was amazed at how many people wrote that they cared and were praying and sending their best wishes. I've since concluded that there is an empathy that all of us carry and spontaneously share. When an experience is very moving, like someone being injured on the street and you rush to help, or you help someone in need in your apartment building, you can't get it out of your mind and you want at minimum to offer words of encouragement. I believe it's inbred. It's innate. And the more severe the condition, which I guess includes liver transplantation, the more it triggers the altruistic response. Crisis brings people together. We can unite around an interest that reaches our humanity. CaringBridge offers that opportunity to unite in compassion.

But the major part of this story for me is the journey: The caregiver part that my wife played throughout all these years since we knew of this disease; Heather's invaluable role; the incredible donor process. I could never have planned it. A power far greater than myself brought everything together.

With Kathy's gift of life I've been able to start over. Now I have to find the strength to deal with the gift day to day. Sometimes all I can and want to do is sit in a chair, but I'm okay with that because I had made my peace with not surviving several years ago, and anything else is far better. I'm back to as close to normal as I have been for years, and I am so glad that I didn't die. I can babysit for my granddaughter, Lucy. I can go more places when I'm finally healed. Every day—*every day*—I am so grateful. I don't care what the weather is, every day is a great day.

I also have a great desire and drive to give back, to do something meaningful. I can't map out what that is yet. I think telling my story to a lot of people over the last several months has certainly fulfilled part of that need.

KATHY: All I know is that I was trying to help save a single person's life. I'd met him when I was in high school. Now I knew his story. I knew his wife. I knew his daughter—and since we'd reconnected after so many years, I knew that Heather had had a child, Paul's granddaughter, Lucy. My brother has a two-year-old son, and he's the highlight of my life. The idea of him ever growing up without knowing his grandfather just broke my heart. Perhaps my inspiration and strength came from wanting Lucy to know her grandfather.

Bad things can happen in life, and at the time, you think, *Why me? Why us? It's not fair.* But somewhere down the road, one hopes to get an answer, and that the answer will be that everything happened for a reason.

Become an Organ Donor

"We make a living by what we get, but we make a life by what we give."

—Winston Churchill

Organ and tissue donations save or improve the lives of tens of thousands of people every year. To become a donor, register with your state donor registry if there is one. Designate your decision on your driver's license and be sure to tell your family about your wishes in the event they must advocate on your behalf.

Visit the US Department of Health and Human Services website, OrganDonor.gov, and the United Network for Organ Sharing (unos.org) to learn more about organ donation and transplantation.

BETH KEATHLEY

How to Die Well

Without actually hearing the "C" word, you know in your heart and deep in your gut that's what the doctor is saying. Your mind races ahead at lightning speed while your knees buckle. My trusted physician was on the phone explaining the results from my CT scan: a "mass" on my pancreas had been found, complicated by its encasement around major blood vessels. He wanted me to go to Moffitt Cancer Center in Tampa for further tests. There, after another CT scan, an endoscopic ultrasound with biopsies (EUS), a PET scan, and several consultations with Moffitt's doctors, I was diagnosed with Stage III/IV locally advanced, unresectable pancreatic cancer. It was not curable, and given pancreatic cancer's typically dismal prognosis—Stage IVs have about six months to live—I faced a now-brief lifetime of debilitating chemo treatments just to gain a few extra months. Some pancreatic patients choose not to treat the cancer at all, just to preserve their quality of life, but I knew I would rather grab ahold of all the time I could.

But this can't be happening, I thought. *I'm not ready! I have plans! I'm fifty-four, just too darned young! I'm graduating from nursing school. I want to get a nursing job. And what will this do to my husband, Rick? How can we cope?*

On the positive side—and with cancer you learn to take those moments whenever and wherever you can find them—my tumor hadn't spread to my lungs or the liver. Yet. And the idea was to keep it that way. My family and friends know that I have a very strong personality. I take nothing lying down. From that moment forward, I was determined to have a positive influence on my physical, spiritual, mental, and emotional healing. Where I could, I would do my part. Where I could not, I would lay it at God's feet.

Moffitt assigned me to Dr. Gregory Springett, a quiet, unassuming, brilliant man who absolutely loves the pancreas and hates cancer. At our first meeting, Dr. Springett gave Rick and me new hope in our war against this most deadly of all cancers. He and his colleagues thought I would be perfect for a clinical-research trial, a cutting-edge treatment that involved being injected with an antibody that finds the pancreatic cancer cells, attaches to them, and then initiates a radio-immunotherapy "kill shot" of radiation. The study also used the standard pancreatic-cancer chemo treatment, commonly called Gemzar, alongside. Only a few dozen patients in the country were participating. Dr. Springett asked if I'd be interested.

"Are you kidding? Where do I sign on?!" Not only could this opportunity possibly be a miracle for me, but I'd also take immense pride in possibly helping future pancreatic-cancer patients. Thankfully the timing was such that I was able to stand proudly with my graduating co-nurses before getting started.

When Lance Armstrong first found out that he had cancer, another cancer survivor told him, "Now you're one of the lucky ones." Actress Gilda Radner, who didn't survive cancer, said, "Everyone should have cancer—if it wasn't for the downside."

Both observations are truths I've come to know with my whole heart. When you face a terminal illness, you get a heightened sense of why you're here. You want it to be important that you're here. You want to leave a legacy. I've grown spiritually. I've learned to stop and smell the roses, to help someone alongside me, to realize I have it pretty darn good.

And yet I no longer desire much of what I once had. So much seems frivolous. For years visiting Israel was on my Bucket List. When I shared with Dr. Springett my uncertainty about being able to take the trip, he said I should go sooner rather than later. "You never know what this disease will do, and you'll never feel better than you feel right now." He understood that for me the trip was not only a vacation but a pilgrimage. It was about more than having fun. I wanted to learn about the country's difficult history.

Rick and I went as part of a group of about fifty people. In Israel we traveled by bus. Unlike so many of my companions, I had lost any desire to shop. I guess the gems were a big bargain, but I wanted memories instead. You can't take gems to the other side, but you can cherish memories and relationships until your last breath.

Facing my own mortality has thrust me into a strange new world that I get to experience with very different eyes, ears, and emotions. Oddly enough, this is a blessing. Simply, I have come to know, and I mean really know, what is important. The rest is noise.

Cancer caused quite a change in me. I used to be more selfish, and certainly ambitious. After I got my bachelor's degree from Virginia Tech in computer science, I spent twenty years in corporate America. I worked for Shell Oil Company and then for American Express. I made vice president. Then one day I'd had enough. I struck out on my own and started a business of recruiting technical people. I was my own boss. I loved that job. When Rick retired, we moved to Englewood, Florida, and I got my real estate license. That was good for a while until the market crashed.

Then I had another epiphany: I'd better get on the wagon and do something truly meaningful. I began with volunteer work with hospice and liked it so much that I became a nurse's aide and worked in a nursing home for a year. That is very rewarding work, but backbreaking as well. I'm in good shape, but at my age I couldn't continue lifting three-hundred-pound women out of bed and getting them dressed in the morning. So I went to nursing school. That's come in handy; now I understand what the doctors are talking about as they prod and poke and do their best to make me better.

The day I arrived at Moffitt, Rick and I found ourselves in the elevator with an older couple. "So which one of you has cancer?" the gentleman asked, his voice literally booming. I'm not shy, but that surprised me. Without thinking, my hand shot above my head. "That would be me!" I announced. How odd it was to hear myself say it, but it was true. I have cancer. The couple asked questions, drawing out my story, and the man told me his. He'd had pancreatic cancer twenty years earlier, but "it went away." I loved the "went away" part. Now he was battling lung cancer. During that short elevator ride, we shared our stories, promising to keep each other in our prayers. I got off the elevator having learned a deeper truth: at Moffitt I had something in common with everyone I met: cancer. From that day forward, while waiting for my appointments, I look for the wristbands that identify a patient. I imagine their story; it's human nature. I know that I am also in the fishbowl and that someone is imagining my story.

This happens to Rick as well. I've often found him surrounded by several caregivers pouring out their lives to him. And yet, while his eyes beg me to save him, I know somehow the experience is healing for him.

Rick is pretty strong. But the pressures we face are great. We have gone through our retirement savings for medical bills. My premiums—mine and mine alone, after my COBRA ended—are about $1,000 a month, and the copay on my Fragmin shots for blood thinning is $400 a month. Rick, who is fifty-nine, had to get a job again for benefits, even though it was a low-paying entry-level position because it's been about ten years since he was in the workforce. His office is ninety miles away in Largo, near Tampa Bay. He works during the week and comes home for the weekend.

Although I miss him terribly, I am happy for him. Rick has connected with new people and he's honing his computer skills again. Working makes him feel better about himself. His whole world no longer revolves around me. I want him to be financially, emotionally, and mentally stable when I'm gone. And I will be gone, so he has to be able to move on with his life.

Relationships, especially marriages, are bombarded with difficult trials and tests, and we all wonder how we'd fare if the "big one" came along. I've known people who've come through serious illness with flying colors, and others not so able to weather the storm. Even though I'm happy that he's established a more independent life, I'm very blessed to have Rick beside me during my ups and downs. The forgotten victim of cancer is the spouse.

I owe so much to him for strength on a daily basis, for him trying to keep life "normal." I know he is worried, weary, and scared, but he inspires me and keeps me laughing even when we want to cry. Rick and I know one thing: it's better to have a partner than to go it alone. If one falls down, the other stands strong.

When Rick is home, we enjoy the quiet times together and find much love and happiness there. But there have been inevitable changes. I have cancer, after all, and we can't be as active as we used to. Because of chemo I can't really be out in the sun, and what else can you do in Florida but be in the sun? So we sold the boat. Rick likes amusement parks, music festivals, parasailing, scuba diving, and fishing. But those have fallen by the wayside, too. Sometimes I just want to lie on the couch and sleep, because that's what the chemo does to me, and I can tell that it makes him sad. It's hard.

Honestly, I am sadder for Rick than I am for myself. Death doesn't feel sad to me, but I can imagine how those I leave behind will feel. I want everyone to be okay. I want my family and friends to understand that I'm not sad about my fate. I won't stop fighting to live, but I've been able to accomplish much in my life. I have always known that we are what we make of ourselves. You're as happy as you want to be.

Most people don't understand. I went to lunch with a friend the other day and told her, "This is the happiest I've been in a long time." She couldn't believe her ears. But I wasn't lying. I now so often feel pure joy. I'm not sure why, but it might have something to do with not believing in depression for most of my life. I understood it as a clinical problem, but I never actually *understood* it. Now I do. I recently had some surgery and afterward had to be cared for by my sisters for three weeks. I could hardly move because of the feeding tube and the IV pole, and suddenly

I realized I felt no joy at all. I felt awful. I didn't care if I woke up or not in the mornings. I regretted the surgery. I was afraid and in the dark. I was angry. I believed that I would never recover to where I'd been before the surgery. All I saw was the downhill. When my younger sister insisted that I had to try and rediscover my joy, I said, "No, I don't."

One day, as soon as I was able, I walked through my neighborhood and heard a bird singing. I felt how wonderful it sounded. All of a sudden, there was joy again. Since then I've only gotten better and better and better. I now realize it was God's plan for me to be depressed in order to fully appreciate my joy. Now I know how low you can go. I know where the bottom can be.

I think this has to do with something called "nearing-death awareness." It's a slow and gradual process that can take months or weeks, but sometimes only days or hours. As people face their own death, they *know* it. They slowly detach from the Earth and become more introspective about what's ahead. You slowly distance yourself. You put space between yourself and your old life. That's what it feels like to me. Some people can even predict the exact time they're going to die, so they want to finish unfinished business. They want closure. They want forgiveness. What people say on their deathbed is not always dementia or the meds kicking in. We should learn to listen and perhaps learn from them.

I feel comfortable now. Peaceful. The roots are in my faith. I can't control my fate, but I know it's going to be okay. I believe that what awaits me on the other side will be magnificent. I'm looking forward to that. I believe that if you believe there is something beyond this world, then you will die a good death. Talk to anybody in hospice and they will tell you that people who have a spiritual side "die well," as they call it, instead of becoming agitated and afraid, holding on to those last minutes. To believe there is nothingness in the beyond makes me incredibly sad. If I thought that, I'd be terrified.

As part of the process, I try to read scripture every morning. Even when I was in nursing school, way before I knew I had cancer, I got up at three in the morning to make sure I did my reading. The habit became even more important after I learned about my disease.

After my initial diagnosis some very religious friends asked me to breakfast. We talked about the cancer, of course. I had sent out a mass e-mail to share the news. "It's really hard," I told them. "I feel as if I've been hit by a train. Well, two trains. The cancer, and people who want to know what's going on even if they also know they should be patient. It's hard to keep up with everybody."

"You should look into CaringBridge," they advised.

I did and it was absolutely perfect.

In fact, after about six months of writing my own online journal, it didn't feel like enough for me. I contacted CaringBridge and asked if there was anything I could do to help them. They were just starting the Amplifier Hub, a place for their volunteers to connect and participate online. The mission is "amplify love, hope and compassion in the world." I wrote a blog post on love, one on hope, and one on compassion. Then they asked me to do a video-log.

Through CaringBridge I've reconnected with people I knew ten or twenty years ago, such as a girl from high school who wasn't even my close friend. Actually, I stole her boyfriend back then, and she knew it, and yet she cared enough and was compassionate enough to reach out and tell me that she'd been following my CaringBridge blog. I was dumbfounded.

I've connected with total strangers who've found my journal. A woman I don't know has been writing in my CaringBridge guest book for about a year. She told me that her brother had pancreatic cancer and was very ill, but was holding on. Then she wrote that he'd passed away, yet he was alert to the end, surrounded by his family. She called it a good death.

I was so struck that I wrote to her saying I was touched, and that her guest-book entries really made my day. She e-mailed me back and revealed that she would read my entries to her brother, and that he knew all about me. That made me cry.

For me, my future has "win-win" stamped on it. I take great delight in believing that heavenly life will be joyful and spectacular. I don't have to worry about trying to control anything. God is in control.

—————

When my clinical trial ended, I had a heart-to-heart conversation about my prognosis with Dr. Springett. I braced myself for what I might hear. He tenderly shared his facts, figures, and data with Rick and me.

The average age of someone diagnosed with pancreatic cancer is around seventy-two. A Stage IV patient's life expectancy is six months. My clinical trial had given me an extra three months—so far. "But you're young and strong, Mrs. Keathley," he said. "I think you will be one to defy averages."

He was right. I've managed to survive for months beyond my doctor's original expectations. What a gift. I didn't think that I would have this much time. But now...now I fear the end is closer. I don't think an infection will get me. I don't think the cancer will spread and shut down my organs. I'm losing weight. After my surgery, I weighed 120 pounds. Now I'm down to 108 pounds. It's only been three months. That is fast. And I'm eating. Boy, am I eating. Dr. Springett has treated thousands of pancreatic-cancer patients and he knows the score. He prescribes ice cream, which makes me laugh. But the weight won't stay on. I don't know how much longer I can go on at this rate, but I won't give up. I've just been accepted into a new clinical trial that will attempt to put some muscle mass and weight back on. Who knows? I might defy all odds and be Moffitt's poster child yet!

Whatever happens, I'm thinking ahead. My memorial and all my final services are laid out and paid for. This book may be out after I'm gone, but right now I'm still here and still hopeful. I really want to live, but I also want to die well.

March 23, 2013, at 4:16 a.m.:
Beth took her last breath yesterday evening. Shortly after she quietly passed, we experienced an incredibly magnificent storm. We are quite certain Beth had something to do with that. Our girl is finally at peace.

—journal excerpt

Acknowledgments

My heartfelt thanks go out to David Rensin, who collaborated on *Hope Conquers All*. To my publisher, Kate Hartson, and the team at Center Street. To Laurie Abkemeier, my talented literary agent, who taught me the ropes.

This book simply would not be possible without a great team behind me at CaringBridge, with special thanks to Melissa Maggio, who kept me on track to make *Hope Conquers All* a reality.

And lastly, my heart soars with gratitude to the brave friends and families that have lived the powerful stories within this book. It is their courage, love, and hope that is the heartbeat within these pages.